Look Ma...
No Hands
An Affectionate Look at Our
Wonderful Tories

Allan Fotheringham

Look Ma...
No Hands
An Affectionate Look at Our
Wonderful Tories

Illustrations by Roy Peterson

KEY PORTER BOOKS

Canadian Cataloguing in Publication Data
Fotheringham, Allan, 1932-
   Look Ma . . . No Hands

ISBN 0-919493-18-1

1. Progressive Conservative Party of Canada - Anecdotes, facetiae, satire, etc. 2. Canada - Politics and government - Anecdotes, facetiae, satire, etc. I. Title.

JL197.P76F67   1983   324.271040207   C83-098999-4

Key Porter Books
59 Front Street East
Toronto, Ontario M5E 1B3

Printed and bound in Canada
by T.H. Best Printing Company Limited

For Douglas Andrew Fotheringham

Contents

Acknowledgments

I am grateful, first of all, to the Progressive Conservative Party of Canada, for supplying the material upon which this autopsy is based. The party's lack of cooperation is greatly appreciated.

I owe a debt to my employer, Southam News, and to *Maclean's* magazine, under whose sponsorship I have gathered the material that forms the basis for parts of this book. Southam News general manager Nicholas Hills has been most generous in allowing time for the production of this tome. It owes much to the imagination and quiet advice of Jennifer Glossop and the assiduous foraging of Beverly Fink Cline. I pay my respects to the special contribution made by Beverley Rockett.

PART ONE

The Yellow Brick Road

1 The Journey Begins

*There were several roads nearby, but it did not take
[Dorothy] long to find the one paved with yellow
brick. Within a short time she was walking briskly
toward the Emerald City. . . . Dorothy did not feel
nearly so bad as you might think a little girl would
who had been suddenly whisked away from her own
country and set down in the midst of a strange land.*
THE WIZARD OF OZ

In February 1976, after the Recessive Convertible Party of
Canada elected someone by the name of Joe Clark as its
new leader, the veteran Vancouver newspaper publisher Hal
Straight was talking on the phone to Conrad Black. The
Toronto establishment man, in his early meanderings to a
hundred million dollars before he was forty, had purchased
Straight's prosperous North Vancouver paper as part of the
Sterling chain.

Straight wondered, over the phone, who this unknown
kid from High River was. "Don't worry," Black assured him.
"We'll get rid of him." Straight chuckles, over lunch one day
in May 1983, and shakes his head. He does not understand
Central Canada, nor does he pretend to. "They'd just elected
the guy. And they're telling me, 'Don't worry. We'll get rid of
him.'"

Jack Pickersgill, the professional imp who decorated the
mischief-making parts of the Liberal party through the Mackenzie King and Lester Pearson years, always said that the
Grits were "the governing party. The Tories are like mumps
—you get them once in your life." Then it's back to the Natural Governing Party.

A descendant of Pickersgill (in the arrogance line) is Tom

13

Axworthy, a refugee from Winnipeg's north end who has a mind as lively as a flea, a necessary attribute considering he is principal secretary to Prime Minister Pierre Elliott Himself. He likes to show up at political conventions with a small lapel button that reads: "Tories are like cream — rich, thick and full of clots."

The Tories, the poor Tories, are none of these things. They are as puzzling as the cure for the common cold, as contradictory as their name, and impossible to dislike. How can you not love a party that changes its leader more often than a cheap hotel changes the sheets, has for 116 years pretended that Quebec does not exist by persisting with unilingual leaders, and replaces (while triumphant in the Gallup Poll) their leader with someone who has never in his life run for public office? Lovable? *Delicious! Delectable!*

Lord Grey, in 1909, called it "the stupid party." That may have been a greater contribution to Canada than the football mug he donated. It is our own native version of the Hatfields and McCoys: Tupper didn't like Bowell; Borden was detested; Meighen was unpopular; Bennett couldn't handle Stevens and quarrelled openly with Manion; Bracken was invisible; Drew imperious; Diefenbaker was knifed by Hees, Nowlan, McCutcheon and Co. before being axed by Camp; Horner savaged Stanfield; Clark was first undermined and then overthrown by Mulroney, who now wants to be the new guy, that beautiful track record before him. There is no fathoming masochism.

The cuddly Tories most resemble, once you get into it, wandering children, innocents, their achievements muddied by their idealism — waifs on The Yellow Brick Road. Ever searching, eyes bright and unsullied by the griefs and responsibilities of power, they stumble on, looking for the the Wizard of Odds.

We have the Cowardly Lion, John Diefenbaker, all bluster and melodramatic jowls, fearful of delegating any authority, frightened of the hobgoblins and ghosts of Bay Street that he imagined hid under his bed each storm-tossed night. All he needed was the courage to face up to his deficiencies

14

— his lack of training for an administrative role or a trustworthy presence, his fearful view that every colleague was a potential assassin, his suspicion that Central Canada viewed him as an unsophisticated rube.

There was the Tin Woodman, Robert Stanfield, a good man in search of a heart that he could display to the public who always stood back from him, slightly mystified about what this uncomfortable-looking chap was doing in an arena where others were bouncing on trampolines, sliding down banisters and pecking nubile nymphs on the cheeks. Mr. Standstill was in constant need of the oil of affection, a man who had been sewn into his emotional underwear since birth and now was being asked to drop his drawers, politically speaking, in public. It did not work and couldn't have. The Tin Woodman rattled when he walked, the wires connecting his voice-box short-circuited so that the sentences came through at the wrong speed on the gramophone.

Jangling along The Yellow Brick Road with them was the Scarecrow, Joe Clark, never in his seven years as leader convincing the electorate that he really had the right stuff. The Scarecrow was on the way to the Wizard of Odds because he wanted a brain. All the while he stumbled, limbs akimbo, in search of coordination, the victim of ambulatory dyslexia.

Who better to lead these souls along The Yellow Brick Road, disguised as Dorothy, than Dr. Foth? Someone, God knows, has to save the country, since the present proprietors are doing such a muck-up of the job. My suggestions for improvement, as is well-known, have been stubbornly ignored in the past. Now we are once more at the crossroads and it seems likely we are about to put the Regrettable Conservationists into power, though they are fully capable, considering their awe-inspiring record, of screwing it up once again.

Conrad Black, who is nominally a Liberal but manages to show up in time for the short strokes at each Conservative leadership vote, says, in the felicitous phrasing typical of him, that the party is made up of "masochists and fruitcakes." Therein lies the secret of this tome. Dr. Foth separates, for you, the masochists from the fruitcakes.

15

Like Dorothy leading the Cowardly Lion, the Tin Wood-man and the Scarecrow down (up?) The Yellow Brick Road, Dr. Foth will conduct the eager reader on a guided tour through the more esoteric byways of the Tory soul. Who are the villains? Why does Bill Davis grin that way? Did Dick Hatfield really bake his cat? Who is the worst MP? And why? Why was Brian Mulroney naked when Joe Clark tried to shake his hand? What happened on The Night Bob Stanfield Got Mad — and Drunk? Who broke the window of the taxi outside the Albany Club? Who is the second-best-dressed woman in Canada? Better still, who is the *first* best-dressed? All those things about Tories you didn't want to know, and couldn't be bothered to ask? Right. They are included. This is the political version of Trivial Pursuit. At the end of the road rests the Tory soul — tortured, guilty, loving the whip, remorseful, and, in the end as in the beginning, childlike.

Finlay MacDonald, the seer of Halifax, who would no more utter an inelegant sentence than not shine his shoes, says the explanation for the dim record of his party is clear. "There are simply not enough Conservatives in this country to elect a government. The only way we can do it, occasion-ally, is to 'borrow' enough dissatisfied Liberals or malcon-tent NDP voters to squeeze in. That's the only way we can achieve power."

The night of June 11, 1983, when the boy from Baie Comeau completed the most audacious raid on democratic politics since De Gaulle rode in from Colombey-les-Deux-Eglises, the esteemed journalist George Bain (who once wrote the most elegantly crafted column ever to grace Ottawa), attempted to hijack a taxi outside the Ottawa shinny rink, where the *coup d'état* had just taken place. Ottawa, it should be ex-plained, among its many disgraces has the worst taxi service — and worst taxis and worst taxi drivers — in Christendom. Foiled and in despair, Bain spotted a lone passenger in a stalled cab and wondered, in polite terms, if perhaps they could share the fare downtown, since every one was badly in need of a drink. The man, in Bain's phrase, "gave me a look as if he had found something moving in his salad." The chap said that anyone who would vote for Brian Mulroney deserved to walk. The taxi sped off.

Past midnight, I boarded an elevator in the Chateau Laurier, the mausoleum that was temporarily aflame with joyous and incensed Tories, on my way up to the suite of the lucky chap who had just inherited this ill-starred flock. The elevator also contained a blowsy woman, her hair the colour of the bottom of the Fraser River, a delegate who had obviously been in a serious bout with the grape and had lost. Ricocheting off the corner walls of the elevator, she curled her lip at poor Dr. Foth and spat out: "*Mulroney.* We'll get rid of him."

2 Sheep for the Slaughter

"There is only one thing in the world I'm afraid of."
"What's that?" asked Dorothy. . . .
"A lighted match," [answered the Scarecrow].

The Tories are carnivorous by habit, omnivorous in their search for victims and, as a result, usually cadaverous in appearance. The party as a whole resembles something out of Dickens: ill-fitting suits, lank of hair and pale of shank, slightly out of sync with the times, mumbling, with last week's egg still on the tie.

Its august members of caucus are either grotesquely over-fed, resembling some refugees from a Hogarthian orgy, or are bow-legged and double-knitted, not suited to modern times. Their MPs appear angry at the world—as they should be, since they so obviously do not fit into it. They are searching for another era, another place, perhaps another role in life.

The anger — or confusion — runs deep. It has been with the party since Confederation. Since they cannot find the real enemy (themselves), the Tories have looked around and seized upon the nearest victim: their own leader. Joe Clark, for all the maudlin remorse, is not a new phenomenon. Since the last century his party has been practising the art, like a frightened mink, of eating its young. Only a party that has been honing its tricks for a hundred years could come up with the skillful self-immolation (portrayed so winningly on colour television) in Winnipeg, in January 1983, followed by the funeral itself in Ottawa in June.

The problem is that this pitiful collection of losers has had only one real leader in its history. When Sir John A. Macdonald was on top, preserved by giggle-juice, the Conservatives formed or led the government in twenty-five out of twenty-nine years. Since his death, it has been all downhill. The Tories have never got over the shock of Sir John A. shucking his gin bottle for the last time. It is a party that has been in mourning for ninety-two years. It is a party of grave-watchers, awaiting the Resurrection.

The Liberals have produced only *one* federal leader in their history, Edward Blake, who was *not* prime minister. They've had only seven leaders in all. The Tories, with more than twice that number, have been led by a series of feckless pursuers of the Peter Principle, each of whom has crashed in his own peculiar way. Clark and his Perils of Pauline was simply the modern replaying of a repetitive Tory theme: nibbled to death by ducks.

Practically every Conservative leader since Sir John A. has been under constant challenge from his own flock. Most of them have had to resign with the snarls of jackals around their ankles. The events of the late 1970s and the early 1980s are not unique: it is a case of Stabbing Revisited. The Tory party is the story of a pack of Brutuses in search of a Caesar. Daggers are always dropping accidentally from their togas (more often than not inflicting serious foot wounds on the owners of the pig-stickers).

From the history of Tory leaders emerges one central theme: it seemed a good idea at the time. The Tories can't even win when they attempt to do the right thing. The tragedy of the hanging of Louis Riel — which has doomed the party in Quebec to this day — was a result of Macdonald's expansive policies toward Western Canada.

The party's strength under his leadership had been its success in bridging the historical differences between Catholics and Protestants, French and English, Quebec and Ontario. Central to Macdonald's plan for national unity was his policy for western development. But once the West was opened to immigration, there was controversy over the rights of the

20

French-speaking, Catholic Métis population that had already settled there.

Riel, of course, escaped to the United States, like Anne Murray after him, following the first Métis uprising in 1869. When sixteen years later he initiated the reprise on the revolution, he was tried for treason and sentenced to the noose. Macdonald wavered but — faced with the feelings of the Ontario Protestant population — decided against intervention. Riel went to the gallows. The party has never recovered.

The departure of leaders (usually with much snarling in the wings) has been ill-timed since then. In the 1891 election, Sir John A. managed to hold onto power despite a loss of ten seats. But he died twelve weeks later, and his party, a precursor of its 1980 equivalent, wasn't prepared for the problem of picking a new leader. The Quebec wing was in a shambles, with prominent members charging one another with corruption, dastardly conduct, mopery and other foul deeds.

The most eminent of Macdonald's surviving colleagues was Sir Charles Tupper. For some reason that has never been explained, the cabinet didn't want him. Next best choice was Sir John Thompson, minister of justice. But because he was a Catholic convert from Methodism, he shielded his eyes, feeling himself unworthy of the task.

The result of this early fumbling (which should have tipped us off) was that the leadership fell to a feckless wonder, Sir John Abbott. He had been mouldering in the Senate, the slumbering body that in later years would be injected with the infectious charisma of the likes of Peter Stollery and Michael Pitfield.

Abbott, who was honest if nothing else, confessed at the time that he had been chosen because he was "not particularly obnoxious to anybody" — proof incarnate that nothing changed in the Tory party from 1891 to 1976.

A king's taster for someone who was to follow him eighty-five years later, everybody's third-choice Abbott was quickly inundated with criticism of his leadership. He had "neither the desire nor the physical ability to give direction."

Thompson, who was leading the party in the Commons,

exercised the real power. By 1892, Abbott was not feeling well and resigned. Tory Number Two had lasted one year.

Number Three, Thompson, lasted two years, having been appointed by the governor-general on Abbott's tired advice. He subsequently went to Britain to be sworn in as a member of the Privy Council. A few minutes after Queen Victoria did the honours at Windsor Castle, he unexpectedly died. Perhaps the occasion did him in.

The zoo act continued. Tupper was once again the pick of the litter but the uppity new governor-general, Lord Aberdeen, sent out to teach table manners to the locals, didn't like the cut of his jib. In addition, proving that Conservatives are consistent, there was the "knot of jealous and feuding individuals in the cabinet, who in pursuit of their own ambitions disregarded the undoubted wishes of the rank and file."

The leadership instead went to yet another member of the Senate, Sir Mackenzie Bowell, Tory Number Four, who looked as if he was out of a Smith Brothers' coughdrop ad. Among his small distinctions, he was a former grand master of the Orange Lodge. He was, as could have been imagined, an unmitigated disaster.

Macdonald's former secretary, Sir Joseph Pope, watched: "Then followed days which I never recall without a blush, days of weakened, incompetent administration by a cabinet presided over by a man whose sudden and unlooked-for elevation had visibly turned his head, a ministry without unity or cohesion of any kind, a prey to the internal dissensions until they became a spectacle to the world, to angels, and to men." *Wonderful!* The only thing they didn't do was move the embassy to Jerusalem.

Bowell was in the great tradition of pseudo-leaders, his rib cage filled with arrows, bananas beneath his spats, tripwires guarding his bathtub. During his first year the cabinet was in a permanent stage of crisis as he procrastinated over the issue of Manitoba's refusal to continue support for separate (that is, Catholic) schools.

While he dithered, in 1895, Sir Charles Hibbert Tupper—minister of justice and son of Bowell's chief rival—resigned.

No sooner was he mollified than three Quebec ministers handed in their resignations. At the opening of Parliament in 1896, half Bowell's cabinet — his "nest of traitors" — announced to the Commons they could no longer serve under his leadership. (Sounding familiar?) This was all part of a Tory plot to force out Bowell and replace him with the elder Tupper.

For ten days Bowell struggled in a death-rattle with a party determined to junk him, twice offering his resignation to the governor-general and twice being refused. The rebels finally forced Bowell to agree that the long-waiting Tupper would take over in the Commons and succeed him at the end of the session.

Sir Charles Tupper, Tory Number Five, was prime minister for all of sixty-nine days. It hardly seemed worth waiting for. In the election of June 1896, the fractious party with its warring elements in Quebec was easy prey for Laurier.

That was the end of the era of Conservative ascendancy in our politics. It would be fifteen years before there was another Tory government. Poor Tupper hung in as Opposition leader until defeated again in 1900, when he resigned.

Tory Number Six — and we are moving right along, aren't we? — was the reluctant Sir Robert Borden, the first leader who had not been a Macdonald minister. Chosen by the caucus when Tupper quit, he had an inauspicious debut. He was defeated in Halifax in the 1904 election but got back to Ottawa through a 1905 by-election in Ontario's Carleton. (In 1908, he was elected in *both* seats, regulations being somewhat more flexible in those days, and chose his old seat.)

Borden appointed a Quebec leader but so undercut him that the chap resigned and was never replaced. Over three sessions Borden, being a Tory, had to confront several intrigues against his leadership.

His flock resented the way he treated them. He was described as distant, moody, imperious, (hello there, Dief) sometimes almost scornful of their worth. He seldom consulted them and, if a caucus was stormy, often would disappear and not call another one that session.

By 1910 the malcontents were moving in for the kill and

Borden offered to resign. He was saved only after considerable debate in caucus, the Tories perfecting the trick that has sustained them for, lo, until the very present — turning their leader on a spit for all to observe.

Having barely escaped execution, Borden, surprisingly, won the 1911 election as the Laurier Liberals split on the reciprocity issue. The Tories were restored to power after fifteen years in the wilderness but the great majority of the new ministers had had no experience in office (hello there, Joe) and the Quebec men proved particularly difficult and unreliable.

In a country split by the conscription issue, a Union government led by Borden took the 1917 election but it was a hollow victory — for the first time since Confederation not a single French-Canadian was elected as a Tory.

His party shattered, an unhappy Borden stayed on until 1920 when Tory Number Seven, Arthur Meighen, assumed the kamikaze seat.

Even on appointment, Meighen was not popular with his fellow MPs and most members of cabinet were opposed to him. As a matter of fact, he got the job only after Borden's first choice, finance minister Sir Thomas White, turned it down. (These lads do have a death-wish.)

The second choice was regarded as reserved, aloof and deficient "in the small personal arts of politics." (Do we hear an echo there, Clarkians?) Within a year his government was crushingly defeated by the Mackenzie King-led Grits and Meighen lost his own seat in Portage la Prairie, regaining it only in a by-election.

Immediately, the jackals were after Meighen and by 1922 he was offering his resignation. One of the persistent and virulent snipers from outside the caucus was Lord Atholstan, publisher of the Montreal *Star*, who wanted a leader more cosy with Montreal railway policy — that is, the CPR.

This fits in with the consistent Tory habit over the decades of viewing power through petty, vainglorious and personally ambitious eyes. The Grits use power to achieve the same ends: they just don't make it so *obvious.*

24

The doomed Meighen was briefly restored to power in 1926 in the King-Byng constitutional fuss, when the Liberal leader was denied by Governor-General Lord Byng a dissolution of the Commons, meaning an election, and had to resign. When Meighen couldn't get the confidence of the House, he had to call the election which King — looking toward Quebec — won easily on the issue of abuse of power by that Brit-appointed Gee Gee.

Meighen immediately resigned and was replaced by the ineffable Hugh Guthrie, interim Tory Number Eight.

In 1927 the Tories chose Number Nine, R.B. Bennett, who had the luck to preside over the Great Depression — wearing a top hat through it all, just as another prime minister wears a fresh rose in his lapel throughout recessions, thus enhancing his appeal with the unwashed. Bennett led the Tories back into power in 1930 (when the Grits were glad to be out of government), but he couldn't handle trade minister H.H. Stevens from Vancouver.

Stevens had made provocative charges — unheard of in those Tory days — about increasing corporate concentration. Bennett, instead of accepting his proffered resignation, gave him the full sway of a royal commission on the charges — and Stevens became a popular hero (where are you, Don Macdonald?).

By the time the insensitive and unbending Bennett finally forced Stevens out of cabinet, there were rumours of a coup against his leadership. Just three months before the 1935 election, Stevens formed his own Reconstruction Party and many Tory workers defected to his cause. The scrapping Tories, naturally, were wiped out at the polls.

Under fire, Bennett quit in 1938. But his likely successor, R.J. Manion of downtown Thunder Bay, had quarrelled openly with Bennett on the floor of the Commons. He published an autobiography criticizing Bennett for his arrogant dealings with cabinet. The two men no longer spoke.

In this chummy atmosphere, the Manion enemies considered Stevens as a challenger to block him. Bennett wanted Meighen and even threatened to run himself. The Manion foes eventually chose Murdoch MacPherson, a former attorney-general of Saskatchewan who had no federal experience whatsoever.

The fated Bob Manion became Number Ten with Meighen, party leader in the Senate, sniping all the way, and Bennett, who finished out his days in Surrey, England, as Lord Bennett, muttering from the underbrush throughout.

When Manion, another hiccup of history, was defeated along with his party in 1940 in an ambush Grit election, he did the gracious thing and resigned in six weeks. The never-to-be-forgotten R.B. Hanson became interim leader and Tory Number Eleven. How soon we lose our memories.

After a delay of more than a year, Hitler's war being considered more important than the never-ending Tory back-biting, it was decided to draft Meighen, who could be considered as Tory Number Twelve, Mark II. He lasted in his second term barely a year.

It took some genius to flub it, but Meighen managed. A by-election had been called in York South to open a seat for him and there was no Liberal opponent. However, Meighen's attacks on Mackenzie King's war policy were such that his only rival, a CCF candidate, won.

We move along swiftly, the names now a blur before us, the blood being wiped from knife after knife, to be replaced by new claret, new curtains concealing new daggers. Do you get the sequence? There is a certain pattern to this collection of assassins that is disguised as a political party.

Meighen had a bright idea. He would recruit as his successor the premier of Manitoba, one John Bracken, a Progressive who had no previous connection with the Conservative Party. This supposedly made him attractive. In such whirlwinds do Tory minds move.

In the 1942 convention, Bracken was opposed by H.H. Stevens, Murdoch MacPherson, Howard Green and John Diefenbaker. (The Toronto-Montreal Establishment that backed Bracken distinguished itself by referring to Dief, in every chance at the microphone in that German-paranoid wartime atmosphere, as "Diefen-backer." The joint chairman of

26

the convention was H.R. Milner, QC, of Edmonton, who barked out "Diefen-backer" in a distinctive way. Dief never forgot. Milner was the leading Conservative in Alberta and he did not become lieutenant-governor, he did not become a senator, he did not become anything.)

The arranged Bracken anointment took place, on the condition that the party change its name to *Progressive Conservative*. Delightful! The *Forward-Backward* Party. All things to all people. It did not work. The ponderous John Bracken, now lucky Number Thirteen, first of all refused to look for the seat in the Commons.

By the time he did, in the 1943 election, the Forward-Backward Party being defeated again, he had lost possible prestige. A fund was established to provide him with a guaranteed annual income if he would retire. It was the first case of a man becoming unknown before he became known. By 1948, having gotten the message himself, Bracken resigned.

The party of losers then decided the secret weapon would be Ontario premier George Drew, he of good suit and strong jaw, whose political record included widely publicized and provocative criticisms of French Canadians. Number Fourteen, if you're counting.

Drew won the leadership on the first ballot over Donald Fleming and Diefenbaker, the latter recalling in his memoirs: "On the night of Drew's victory, I went up to his suite in the Chateau Laurier. They were celebrating. I was an intruder. I went to congratulate him. I walked into that gathering and it was as if an animal not customarily admitted to homes had suddenly entered the place."

Defeats through the 1949 and 1953 elections at the hands of the St. Laurent government finally focused the growing restiveness in the party — aimed at the small inner circle that controlled positions of influence. With that Chinese water-torture the Tories have perfected as the method of destroying their leaders, the stress on Drew grew until, in mid-1956, he collapsed from emotional and physical exhaustion.

At last, we come to our modern period of insurrection, rebellion, intrigues and plots. Even John Diefenbaker, the popular hero picking up the pieces from Drew on a first-ballot victory in 1956, had plotters attempting to block him. Those who already perceived some of the Dief's weaknesses attempted to recruit an alternative, since they didn't consider his rivals, Donald Fleming and Davie Fulton, to be of sufficient stature. They even went so far as to approach Beverly Baxter, an expatriate Canadian who was a Conservative member of the British Parliament. Among his other sins, Baxter wrote a column for *Maclean's*.

Diefenbaker, as Tory Number Fifteen, gave his party its first government in twenty-two years when he won his minority in 1957. He was tolerated — though never really accepted — by the party brass as long as he was a winner. Once he started down the slippery slope in 1962, the hatchets were honed, Bowell's latter-day "nest of traitors" eventually reappearing, the Hees *et al.* loyalists who trumpeted their fidelity at one caucus turning on the paranoid Man from Prince Albert soon after and destroying him.

Dief took his revenge by niggling and naggling at the valiant but confused Robert Stanfield, Number Sixteen, behind his back and to his front. Jack Horner took *his* by shivving Joe Clark, Number Seventeen, until his frustration took him into the arms of the Liberals and the Canadian National.

The surprising Clark resiliency may have come from his simply reading the history of his party. In retrospect, the fanatics, the bats, the bellicose, the loonies and the liverish who plagued him may be a mere shadow of what has gone before.

As Number Eighteen, Brian Mulroney undoubtedly will find out.

3 The Cowardly Lion

"What makes you a coward?" asked Dorothy. . . .
"It's a mystery," replied the Lion. "I suppose I
was born that way. All the other animals in the
forest naturally expect me to be brave, for the Lion is
everywhere thought to be the King of Beasts. I
learned that if I roared very loudly every living thing
was frightened and got out of my way. . . . As soon as
they hear me roar they all try to get away from me,
and of course I let them go."

On June 11, 1957, I was walking about London. Newly arrived, a tad of twenty-four, beginning a three-year residence, as awed as any colonial raised on the history of the most interesting town on earth, I decided to explore on foot for an hour or so.

I walked along Hyde Park from my digs in Notting Hill Gate, down the fringe of the Mayfair gilt, along Piccadilly, and headed east. At Green Park, the shocking-red newspaper callboards shouted a morning message: TORIES IN CANADA AHEAD! A little flicker in the heart of one strolling Canadian went on, like a barbeque starter. A spring came into the step. John Diefenbaker, the outsider, indeed had a chance after all.

Along the Strand, the street editions of the most competitive newspaper market on the globe screamed further bulletins: CANADIAN CONSERVATIVE SURGE CONTINUES. Seduced by the walkable byways that soothe the eye and delight the feet, I traced the Thames. The callboards became more frenetic. In that era when Mother England was beginning to feel neglected, here was one unregenerate lover of Over 'Ome, even though he did have a German name, gaining power across the water.

I tarried in a pub over brown ale and good cheddar, only to

emerge to more cheering headlines: DIEFENBAKER GUARDS LEAD. It was a great day to be a Canadian, especially a Western Canadian. For the rest of that balmy London day, I watched the world I had left unfold on the callboards as the editions rolled on through the evening papers.

I simply walked the day away, aches erased on the euphoria of the bad old Grits at last being overthrown by what seemed to be a faultless champion from the fastness of Prince Albert. I learned London on foot on a day that made Canadians, both home and abroad, feel more proud, more Canadian.

There was a feeling of exuberance, shared with other Canadians encountered in London in succeeding days, that can be equated only with the pride felt during the heady days of Montreal's Expo 67.

On June 23, 1957, just fifty-three hours after his first cabinet meeting, John Diefenbaker flew to London for the Commonwealth Prime Ministers' Conference. The jingoistic *Daily Express*, owned by Lord Beaverbrook, had been doing absolute nip-ups over this brilliant new champion of the monarchy and of all the old ties held dear by the Beaver. The morning Diefenbaker arrived, the headline in the *Express* proclaimed in startling type as if it were the Second Coming, emblazoned across the top of page one: DIEF THE CHIEF ARRIVES! That label, which was to follow him through his tortuous career as Canadian prime minister, was the invention of a grizzled and anonymous Brit deskman soaked in pencils and no doubt gin on the *Daily Express* newsdesk. It may have been the Beaver's most memorable gift to our folklore.

Diefenbaker had already become a bit of a legal legend in Canada through the highly-publicized court battles that he shrewdly chose. The first of these was his defence of Alfred John Atherton, a twenty-two-year-old CNR telegrapher charged with manslaughter after a train wreck at Canoe River, British Columbia, which had killed seventeen Korea-bound soldiers. Diefenbaker, who had had to pay fifteen hundred dollars to join the closed-shop union of B.C. lawyers for the privilege of defending the 1950 case, discovered early in the

30

trial that the soldiers had been in wooden coaches while the officers on the train were in secure steel cars.

To Dief's further delight, the prosecutor, the B.C. deputy attorney general, turned out to have the name of Colonel Eric Peppler, KC. At every possible opportunity, Dief laid on the references to "Colonel," all the while hammering away at the contrast between the officers encased in their safe steel cars and the men dying in wooden coaches.

As always, Dief had placed a friend in the gallery to watch the reactions of the jury. When his spy, a man named Snow, reported the disgust on the faces of one juror in the front row, a First World War veteran, and another in the back row, a Second World War vet, Dief knew he was home free. He won an acquittal for the young telegrapher and marched back to Ottawa to the plaudits of the nation.

He had established in the public mind, through the trials in which he was always on the side of the underdog, that here was a man of the people and for the people.

The trial was a key to understanding John George Diefenbaker and explaining why this strange man, so reviled by political observers and almost everyone in Ottawa, became such a mythic figure in our politics. He had a touch for human emotions which never deserted him even on those latter days when he verged on becoming a caricature of himself.

From the start, as an outsider, not trusted in the Commons by either the Tories or the Liberals, Diefenbaker used his gifts with the language to make his reputation. The ordinarily sedate Liberal finance minister James Ilsley once grew so irritated at a stagey Dief harangue that he shouted at him: "Don't become so intoxicated with the exuberence of your own verbosity! Get away from this sophomoric invective and adolescent abuse!"

With the words, as journalist Gordon Donaldson put it, "came the punctuation, the distracting grunt, the terrible pause, the accusing finger, the massive head in disdainful profile." Dief in full flight had the mannerisms of a Rudolph Valentino, nostrils aflame with passion after some helpless damsel — as in one of those old silent movies seen late at night. Diefenbaker once threw himself on the floor of the Supreme Court of British Columbia, clutching his throat to show how a murder had been committed. Little wonder that John Kennedy and his rep-tie set from Harvard thought him a mountebank, an outdated poseur.

The best description of the Diefenbaker liberty with the language was given in the House in 1958, after he had been PM for almost a year. Alistair Stewart, the Socialist MP from Winnipeg, said:

> The relationship between the Prime Minister and the cliché is not that between master and servant; it is that of master and slave, because he beats these clichés and bruises them, sets them dangling before us, and then, having bludgeoned them with such violence, he buries their bleeding bodies in the pages of *Hansard.* If we want to find out what has been happening, we have to disinter these victims of verbosity and when we conduct a post mortem we find that nothing has been happening.

The man who invented this slippery speech form actually explained it once during the 1963 campaign to the Toronto *Star*'s Val Sears, then going through one of his many incarnations as Ottawa bureau chief for the paper (which changes the occupants of that post faster than Italy goes through prime ministers). "You know," Dief told Sears, "sometimes I think of a clever phrase during a speech and I start to say it and then I stop and think 'that's taking me down a road I don't want to go' and change direction, or I don't finish the sentence. That way, they can't pin me down. They say: 'Diefenbaker said so-and-so,' and they go and look it up and there's a turn somewhere. They can't catch me out."

Dief's mangled attempts at franglais, of course, were legendary. His finest hour came when, in a speech in Quebec that was carried province-wide on radio, he manfully attempted his mandatory few sentences in French. What his speech writers had given him was, *"J'espère que mes voeux seront appreciés."* (I hope my good wishes will be well received.)

How it came out, in the famed Prince Albert pronunciation, was: *"J'espère que mes veaux sauront après shiés.* (I hope my calves will know how to shit afterwards.) Radios fell off the tables all over Quebec. The Tories, as you know, have never recovered there since.

The franglais, naturally, works both ways. Camillien Houde, the gargantuan Montreal mayor, was once asked to do the ceremonial kick-off at a McGill football game. He did the required duty, then grasped the microphone and announced enthusiastically that he had enjoyed the experience and if he were asked back in the future he would be glad "to kick all your balls off." I digress.

Diefenbaker was, of course, a terrible prime minister, mystified by decision-making, obsessed by his suffocating inferiority complex, happy only when appealing to the public for succor. But he had a gift — a gift shared by few others — of spotting totems, symbols, rituals that strike a nerve. He may have been a lousy leader but he was excellent litmus paper.

In the Commons galleries, on those days when he deigned to appear, the public tensed when he stood, hands on hips, spurious indignation rising from him in sheets. With a phrase he could capture a corner of Page One — an ability denied the next two men who succeeded him. He had a connection cord to the public, a nerve end for simplistic issues — a Royal mailbox, a Mountie, a railway telegrapher. He was an anti-Ottawa man, which is why he failed as PM and why he survived into his eighties as a tribune of the people.

Like all men of surpassing ego, the Chief had few close friends, only acolytes. (Though he was loyal: both the lawyer who assisted him in that railway wreck trial and the two benchers who eased through his B.C. licence were appointed judges.) He was always the solitary man. Betty Davis, a friend of Edna, his first wife, told author Simma Holt of the Diefenbakers sitting in the bleachers at the Saskatoon railway station during the 1939 visit of King George and Queen Elizabeth.

Once the royals left the platform, the crowds surged toward the stage.

> I believe the Queen came down to speak to the veterans and Edna said, "Come on, John. Let's go down there." John would not go and Edna said, "Come on, Betty, let's go." We were within a couple of feet of the Queen and could hear all the conversation. . . . When we looked up in the bleachers, I saw John sitting all by himself. He had not moved. It is a picture I will never forget. I thought to myself that is the classic and real John Diefenbaker — a loner who would not move out of himself even to get close to his Queen.

The voracious Holt, a good newspaper reporter who had known Diefenbaker for the five years she served in the Commons, after his death rummaged around in the story of his first, twenty-two-year marriage for her book, *The Other Mrs. Diefenbaker*. She found that

> John never really learned to be "one of the boys." No matter how determined he was to change from a natural recluse to a social person, he often balked at the last moment. Sometimes it was self-indulgence; he wanted to do what he loved most — hide away in his bedroom and read. Sometimes it was outright fear of being with people. There were times, family and friends said, that John would even cross the street rather than have to face someone and get involved in conversation.

In that, there is more than a little trace of Pierre Trudeau and Joe Clark.

Historians might ponder the fact that Dief — like R.B. Bennett, like Laurier, like Borden, like King — was childless. As such, of course, obsessed with self. (How much of the character of this prim country is the product of such incomplete, driven men who have ruled us as prime minister?)

Dief was a politician apart, a man who, as Peter Newman

put it, "like P.G. Wodehouse's fictional butler, Jeeves, entered any room 'as a procession of one.'"

He was also, like so many self-obsessed men, a momma's boy. Virginia O'Brien, a friend of the family, remembers:

> Mrs. Diefenbaker (mother Mary) was a very strong character. I certainly understand what bothered Edna so much. As soon as John came into his parents' home he was mother's boy, not Edna's husband. I remember John would stretch out on the chesterfield — yes, as a full-grown, middle-aged man — with his head in his mother's lap and she would stroke him and run her hands through his hair. Edna would actually throw up. Mickey and I were over for tea several times and we saw it.

Mickey O'Brien, a legendary Vancouver advertising figure, was one of the chief pushes in making Dief party leader.

He was many things — among them, by the way, not a teetotaller. "He had the odd drink. I know. I served it to him myself," says Frank Swanson. Now the retired publisher of the Calgary *Herald*, Swanson was once the Ottawa *Citizen*'s press gallery man and used to attend the Diefenbakers' Sunday-night dinners in their small Ottawa apartment along with such as Arthur Blakely of the Montreal *Gazette* and the Toronto *Telegram*'s Peter Dempson. Swanson was always asked to be bartender. "He would say: 'Pour me one.' It was always Scotch and water."

By the time Diefenbaker finally achieved his dream of becoming prime minister his solitary nature had been turned into paranoia. The Liberals, cynical even then, harassed him by gerrymandering his seat out of existence. They even converted the house next door to his Prince Albert residence into a foster home for unwed Indian mothers (considered disgraceful in those days).

At sixty-one, when he took power, he was too old to learn the gifts of organization and delegation he'd never needed as an individualist lawyer and barnstorming defence attorney from a small town in northern Saskatchewan. Just as power corrupts, lack of power can corrupt too. The slights had been too deeply embedded, the imagined enemies too real. The bitterness of 37 years was too much.

What Dief did have was grass-roots appeal. When he was elected in 1957 he went across the country by train, meeting the *families* of every provincial Conservative cabinet minister. A Winnipeg woman, with wonder still in her eyes, remembers as a twelve-year-old being taken by her politician father down to the train, and seated on Dief's knee, while Olive brought candies for all the gathered children. Peter Newman remembers seeing, as a bareheaded Dief addressed a crowd in the rain in Penticton in B.C.'s Okanagan Valley, some of his listeners deliberately closing their umbrellas.

He was our first and only grass-roots leader. Stanfield never had grass roots — and didn't know how to spell it. Clark sincerely believed he had an affinity for grass roots, but he was never able to demonstrate it. Mulroney, for all his supposed corporate slickness, is perhaps the nearest to the grass roots of all recent Tory leaders; no one else has come from such a non-genteel background.

In the end, John Diefenbaker became the victim of his own oratorical gifts, the hired mouthpiece of the courtroom who treated the populace as a jury that could be conned and swayed. He was, as Tommy Douglas put it, a "larynx thinker, visceral in this thinking." He had to think out loud, with his voice, to get the effect and the reaction.

In the end, he was destroyed by his inability to do anything but speak. The quintessential scheming Grit, Jack Pickersgill, who made a dining-out profession of debunking Diefenbaker, maintained that Dief believed that when he said something he had done it. Thus during the Diefenbaker regime, Canadians saved themselves by building fallout shelters, liberating the Ukraine and "getting tough with the Yanks."

Pickersgill, as a personal hobby, loved to track down some of Dief's wilder exaggerations and extensive liberties with the truth. His favourite is the tale of how Diefenbaker, always seeking a place for himself in the history books, attended the founding conference of the United Nations in San Francisco in 1945. The way Dief told it, he desperately wanted a memento of the occasion and so attempted to retrieve a cigarette package tossed aside by Jan Christiaan Smuts, who was prime minister of South Africa and one of the world's prime statesmen at the time. Dief's story-telling gifts were at his best when he described how he furtively retrieved the treasure, trying to hide his scavenging from the TV cameras.

Pickersgill, chortling in glee, points out that in 1945 there was no television. And Jan Christiaan Smuts didn't smoke.

Diefenbaker was brought down, in the end, by the decision-makers of Central Canada who concluded that he was uncontrollable and that he must be disposed of. But that same Central Canada helped to *create* him by fuelling regional resentments with its Fortress Ontario mentality, its contempt for the hinterland that sustained its very wealth. Diefenbaker was the product of those resentments and suspicions toward the prosperous manufacturing centre of the country. He represented a region and a regional feeling; he was assaulting the castle from outside.

Dalton Camp, possibly the most interesting character never to have fully penetrated the Canadian political system, was the Trojan Horse used to unseat The Chief. As president of the party, bald beyond his years, he initiated the unseemly idea of a leadership review (ending up, 17 years later in 1983, decrying the monster he had created, in defence of the beleaguered Joe Clark).

No one will ever know (unless Camp eventually publishes the long-promised second volume of his elegant memoirs, *Gentlemen, Players and Politicians*) whether he fancied himself as the successor. He did offer his body and his brain before the voters. The latter commodity was deemed too esoteric. He relegated himself, with grace, to New Brunswick and the typewriter. One suspects greater good resulted.

Instead of a lone Brutus, such is the nature of the Tories that they always had a convenient supply of bodies to do in the leader who reacted nervously at every rustle of the cur-

37

tains. George Hees, proclaiming fealty in his cheerleader's fervour at one caucus meeting, was easily lured into insurrection at the next. Quebec's Leon Balcer and Bay Street's Senator Wally McCutcheon were part of the crew planning Dief's walk to the plank. (McCutcheon and Nova Scotia's George Nowlan used to sample the rye in the morning period. Rye was always the Tory drink then, for a reason. You couldn't afford *Scotch*.)

Camp did not have to orchestrate the night of the long knives. The caucus, as by rote, the computer going back to Bowell and Tupper, remembered the program. Camp, like the man directing the Boston Pops, could do it all from memory.

John Diefenbaker was a tribune of the people because he gave promise, for a short while, to the dream that a Lone Stranger, riding out of nowhere, could indeed buck Bay Street and the Rideau Club and Rockcliffe and the bullet-proof swivel servants. Of course, aided by his own self-apparent defects, he never had a chance to penetrate the case-hardened Ottawa mentality. There is nothing so ferocious in its defence mechanisms as a town threatened by a new idea, carried by an unknown quality.

He was not totally to blame. The selfish centrifugal forces that have ruled for too long such a disparate country contributed greatly to his paranoia. History will be kinder to him, one suspects, than the professional mockers such as Pickersgill, a man who wormed his way into the power structure that Dief tried to defy.

The interpretation of him, to the Canadian public, was done by journalists based on the Ottawa-Toronto-Montreal circuit, who basically feel offended that someone not of the structure can burst onto the political scene. Dief epitomized the distrust felt in this country for the Ontario power circuit. As such he has never been fully understood, has never been explained sympathetically.

The pros sneered and the press sneered but the Chief in his fading years moved about the country like a battleship, enjoying each wave he made. His deadly tongue was still feared — especially within his own party. He never forgave a slight, nor forgot.

What, sir, is the secret of surviving into one's eighth decade?

"To make a decision, and to leave it behind. Olive taught me that: 'Whatever is, is. What is done, is done.' Never hold a grudge."

In fact, as his life demonstrated, he was the world champion grudge-holder. He never forgot a single one. That, too, is human.

Dief sat in his office one day a few months before his death in 1979, in quiet enjoyment of his own notoriety, head shaking with the riveting fascination of a metronome. At eighty-two, the famous silver and black rivulets of hair still sprang from his forehead like the bolts of lightning in those early Duncan Macpherson cartoons, the eyes of evangelical intensity bulging in horror at the onset of a punch line.

He was the raconteur supreme, slowly rearranging the mental furniture, each anecdote sculpted in elaborate sentences, moving sedately toward the denouement — rather reminiscent of the forty-nine-year-old Gordie Howe casually, carefully, inexorably boring in on goal — holding off interruptions with a cautionary eyebrow, a threatening finger.

Why, sir, did you feel it necessary to denigrate in the third volume of your memoirs so many dead people who can't answer back?

The wattles shook with suppressed glee. "They have had their say. They have given their versions. Now I am having mine."

It was a staggering list of incompetents that he had stumbled upon. In the book, Lester Pearson comes out a cheat. George Hees a blubbering fool. Wallace McCutcheon an incompetent turncoat. Douglas Harkness, whose resignation was "not of great importance," allegedly needed liquid lubrication before resigning. He is savage to Davie Fulton. John Robarts is unfaithful. Ged Baldwin is petulant. Even Grattan O'Leary somehow comes out a traitor. It is literary necrophilia.

He had that incessant mean streak. I remember him in his office in the Centre Block, chortling and beckoning his acolytes to gather closer while he explained that the election of Joe Clark was understandable. He delivered the punch line with the measured cadence of a Gregorian chant: "This is" — chortle, snort — "the International" — chuckle, hoist of eyebrows — "*Year of the Child!*" His jowls shook with glee, his eyes bugging for effect.

He was a good actor as a politician who turned, eventually, into simply an actor. He ended his days in Ottawa as he began them, the outsider, still searching for a stage.

4 The Tin Woodman

The Tin Woodman knew very well he had no heart,
and therefore he took great care never to be cruel or
unkind to anything.
   "You people with hearts," he said, "have
something to guide you, and need never do wrong;
but I have no heart, and so I must be very careful.
When Oz gives me a heart of course I needn't mind
so much."

Robert Stanfield's problem was that he was seen as a solution to what had gone before. He was to be everything that Diefenbaker was not — a loyal party man, an administrator, someone who could be trusted, someone who could attract the voters. He was looked on as the "answer" to the problems of the troubled Tories.

But no one ever bothered to look at the features, the characteristics, of the man himself and contemplate whether he fitted into what was supposed to be a modern federal party. On reflection, considering his background of discreet family wealth, his life spent in one of the more slow-moving areas of the country, he was most unfit for the role assigned him. He was a courteous man loosed among randy opportunists, hard-eyed hucksters and ambitious con men.

In his Harvard Law School days, he lived in the same rooming house for three years. The only way other students detected that he had substantial family money was that he occasionally bought a 78 rpm record, which, in those days, cost ten dollars.

The first time he met Stanfield, Dalton Camp remembers, "Well, I thought, at least he's not pretty. Long-headed, with shrewd, heavily lidded eyes (a slight cast in one), a long nose, and full mouth. All else was elbows and knees."

Much later, after he had become accustomed to the Stanfield style, Camp said, "If you'd hooked onto Stanfield in 2000 B.C. and said, 'Look, Bob, I've got a great idea here. It's a circle and you put it on a cart and it's a wheel,' he would say in that slow voice of his, 'Well, I'm not going to make a speech about it until I see it. And until I see it, I'm not going to buy it.' That's the way he was."

It was another old-time Nova Scotia pal who observed, "This guy has the makings of another Abe Lincoln. He's going to be hard to elect, but if we ever get him elected, they'll never get him out."

In Ottawa, however, he had his problems, mainly connected to his background. He was a provincial premier (no premier has ever become prime minister) with a patrician upbringing. The reticent gifts that made him such a successful premier of Nova Scotia for eleven years were out of date when transferred to the national stage just when the teeny-bopper-kissing Pierre Trudeau, the Prince of the Shopping Plazas, came along.

He had a "provincial" mentality, a man grafted onto the federal scene too late in life. In Nova Scotia, politics was a family affair.

Journalist Geoffrey Stevens, Stanfield's greatest fan, tells the story about the new Roman Catholic priest who moved into a small Nova Scotia town in the days when television was still a novelty. The priest, as became quickly known, had the only TV set in town. At provincial election time, several men of the parish, fierce Liberals, approached the priest after mass one Sunday, asking whether they could drop by election night.

As the results poured in, his guests waited impassively until the votes were announced for their small community; eighty-seven for the Liberal candidate, forty-six for the Conservative. Instead of being overjoyed, as the priest expected, his parishioners sat in sullen silence. "But Alec," one of them finally said to his mate, "how can this be? There are eighty-seven Liberals in town, but everyone knows there are only forty-five Conservatives." To a man, they turned and stared icily at the priest.

Stanfield came from the kind of old-money background where privilege was accepted but not talked about. It required that you make a virtue out of being old shoe. He shunned limousines. He refused to move into a suite—even if, as happened one night in Montreal in 1972, his hotel accidentally booked him into a single room with an unorthodox bed that folded into the wall. "I had this horrible premonition," confessed a Stanfield functionary, "that I would come in in the morning and find no Stanfield — just a tangle of arms and legs sticking out of the wall."

Luck never followed him. In 1958 he went to England and met the Queen. Since it was spring, he travelled to one of the great sporting events of that funny little country, the Epsom Derby. (Chesterton said the average Englishman was not so much upset about the inequality among men as the inequality among horses.) He decided to put a small wager on a darkhorse, Hard Ridden. Before he could get the bet down, he was called away to the telephone and missed the post call. Hard Ridden won the Derby, at 18-1.

He would never complain. He accepted life. Because he was such a correct product of a taciturn society, he seemed cool and uncommunicative to those under him. He was respected, but not admired or loved. Members of his staff found him frustrating to work for, and were forever waiting for decisions that seldom came. In 1968, facing the challenge of the trendy Trudeau, a bright twenty-two-year-old recruit from Western Canada in the Stanfield office presented him with a proposal for youth involvement in the coming election. It sat for a year on Stanfield's desk.

"RLS," says one former staffer who loved him but despaired of him, "was so aloof that people felt uneasy around him, but he was so decent he came to be regarded highly for that quality." It is not a quality that generally leads to election. He was the Calvin Coolidge of Canadian politics, rationing words like gumdrops. ("I just bet my companions I could make you say more than two words," gushed a woman who rushed up to Silent Cal at a cocktail party. "You lose," he replied.)

Stanfield, in fact, was Camp's second choice as the man to replace Diefenbaker. Convinced that Stanfield meant it when he said that he "would rather go ski-jumping" than move to the Ottawa scene, Camp went after Manitoba premier Duff Roblin.

Roblin, terrified at having his Western Canadian support eroded by the thought of being associated with the man who had brought down the Prairie ikon figure of Diefenbaker, shied away. Camp, frustrated, then convinced Stanfield it was his patriotic "duty" to rescue the party. Stanfield, his integrity being questioned, gave in. Roblin, once rid of Camp, then came in the race too late with too little. This is the way the Tory world moves — to a strange beat.

Unaccustomed to life in the fast lane of Central Canada, Stanfield became the captive of the Eddie Goodmans, the Dalton Camps, the Norm Atkins. They were the masters of Toronto's own brand of slick, and this humpbacked, dark-suited, halting-voiced gentleman from the old school, an old province, with old money, was betwixt and between, resembling a man playing at Wimbledon in long whites, continuously being caught on the wrong foot.

Robert Stanfield did not *enter* a room. He oozed into it and sometime after the event you became aware of him. In public appearances he always reminded me of Carl Sandburg's *The fog comes/On little cat feet/It sits looking/Over the harbour and city/On silent haunches/And then moves on.*

I talked with him one day in his Ottawa office and he was actually doodling, the most vigorous action I'd seen from him since he ate the banana. By the final weeks of the 1974 campaign, the word was that Tory strategists were contemplating surrounding Mr. Stanfield with an electric-eye detector so that for the remaining interval until the election no one would be allowed to hand him a funny hat, foot-long hot dog, baseball bat or Frisbee. If they did, the detector would make the object in question fall to the ground, where one of his aides would stamp it to death.

44

The packaging of this lumpish product, of course, did not work, since the public comprehension of him was barely six months old before Trudeau captured all eyes and headlines early in 1968.

The scene is the flagstone patio of The Oaks, the Robert Stanfield home in Halifax, the day after the debacle of the 1968 election. Stanfield and the Tories, of course, have been buried under Trudeaumania, and the pallbearers — Finlay MacDonald, Toronto's Fast Eddie Goodman, Gene Rheaume, Flora MacDonald and a few others — have gathered for lunch. The gloom is hedge-high.

Suddenly Fast Eddie, the Bay Street corporation lawyer, leaps to his feet. "I've got it!" he cries. The mourners look at him strangely. Goodman is a short, compact man, all quick motions and urgent signals. He has a lisp and he talks in staccato bursts, a riveting spectacle when his motor is revved up.

"I've got it!" an excited Goodman exclaims. "We start right now, building for the next election. We start a rumour. We plant it. Get it going right across the country. It will sweep the population."

The Stanfield entourage gazes puzzled at the antics of Fast Eddie, who by now is dancing with excitement. "Here it is," he whispers. "This is the rumour: Bob Stanfield comes home for nooners!" Mary Stanfield laughs so hard she falls off her chair into a rose bush.

There are some things you should know about Bob Stanfield, who was with us for nine years in Ottawa, verging near the top but never quite making it. You should know that one day in Vancouver, after a press conference (that had died because of his dullness), a few of us stayed behind to have a drink with him in his hotel suite. One of the group was Jack Webster, The Mouth that Roared of Vancouver broadcasting fame, who is instant showbiz in any gathering over two persons.

Webster is a legend in his own mind, a man who makes $300,000 a year (with a chauffeur and five months' holiday) and is a dominating, entertaining raconteur — especially of stories revolving around himself. He was into one of his tales and just mounting full steam when Stanfield gently skewered him with a remark about Webster's self-importance. There was a large hiss as the air went out of Webster. He wound himself up for a second time and launched forth. Just before the punch line came another Stanfield shaft. There was another loud hiss of air. A third time Webster pumped himself up. A third time an incisive, deadly, precise Stanfield line punctured him completely. The ineffectual Bob Stanfield, politics' worst communicator, completely destroyed the toughest talker in journalism. In such close company he was delightful.

The number-one drinking event in Ottawa, about which the public never hears, is the off-the-record parliamentary press gallery annual dinner. Each year that he was there, Stanfield's droll speech from the head table completely overshadowed Trudeau's. His self-deprecating wit ("Am I speaking too fast for you?"), adroitly timed one-liners and perfectly chosen insults made Trudeau, woodenly reading his gag-filled script, sound like a Rotarian.

At the dinner following his 1974 defeat, Stanfield rose and began his ponderous introductions. "Your Excellency," he said, turning to Governor General Jules Leger, "Prime Minister, Mr. Broadbent, Mr. Chairman, ladies and gentlemen — and Doug Ball." The place collapsed. It was an in-joke of magnificent self-deprecation, since Doug Ball was the photographer who took that famous campaign shot of Stanfield fumbling a football, a devastating cameo that was widely credited with encouraging his defeat. There are Tories still bitter over the selective way newspapers played that picture, since Ball had supplied Canadian Press (which distributed the photo) with other shots of a surprisingly graceful Stanfield catching and passing the football. It's a debate still argued in press clubs, but only Stanfield had the sense of humour to handle it.

This is the same man, remember, who sent Christmas cards, signed by himself, to newspapermen who all year brutally chopped him into tiny pieces and then toyed with the remains. It is extremely hard to dislike such a man.

The public never saw Stanfield's emotions on display — and assumed he had none. A glimpse was seen, however, on the final day of the futile 1968 campaign, when an exhausted Stanfield boarded his lumbering campaign plane in Belleville, Ontario, for the flight home to Halifax and the obvious results from the ballot box. He had travelled forty thousand miles in fifty-one days in an increasingly useless crusade while the press and the public went ga-ga over this rich, sexy bachelor called Trudeau.

While reporters filed their last stories, Stanfield settled into a bottle of Scotch. Once aloft, he marched into the press section, sat down beside the *Globe and Mail*'s Geoff Stevens and took off on a bitter attack on the press. The scribes, astounded and delighted at the passion of a Stanfield they had never seen before, gathered in stunned awe.

The Tory leader ripped into Trudeau with great contempt. Robert Stanfield, in truth, was swacked. To show that Trudeau was not the only politician who had ever read a book, Stanfield quoted lengthy passages from De Tocqueville and talked knowledgeably about music and theatre. There was one stop in Moncton, where Stanfield staggered from the plane to deliver a few words for the local candidate — except he couldn't remember his name.

When he reached Halifax, he was driven home and the accepted version is that when Mary Stanfield opened the door of The Oaks, her husband fell flat on his face at her feet. "That's the last thing the country needs," she cracked, "another Sir John A. Macdonald." Next morning as the Stanfields entered a church basement to vote, Mary Stanfield turned to Geoff Stevens. "What did you do with my Bob last night?" she demanded. There was something in her eye, as Stevens recalls. "It might have been a twinkle."

Can there have been anyone more loyal than Stanfield? He was battered by the fickle voters for three elections — just before they changed their minds and decided to take a short-lived flyer on the kid from High River of whom Stanfield said, after experiencing him as an aide, that "he should seek a future elsewhere, being too twitchy and insecure for that trade." He put up stoically for years with the backstage mischief of Dief. He even endured Jack Horner. His first wife was killed in a car crash. His second wife died of cancer.

Try to understand the determination and patience of a man who at age fifty-three (inarticulate even in English, remember) painfully and painstakingly set about the task of learning French so he could more adequately represent both sections of this truncated country. And then to witness, as his reward, the neanderthal portion of his party carving him up behind his back after the 1974 election defeat because he "wasted" too much of his time learning Canada's other language.

In 1979, when he was finally out of the limelight, happily married again and gardening in Ottawa, he was dragged out of his dignity to get Joe Clark's cookies out of the fire by posing as the man who would do an "exhaustive study" of the Jerusalem embassy fiasco. The accident-prone Clark had waited barely twenty-four hours after being sworn in to plunge his boot into his mandibles and boast that he would indeed move the Canadian embassy from Tel Aviv to Jerusalem. The resulting fallout from business and diplomatic circuits had the Clarkians reeling on their heels within a week of taking office.

Stanfield, maintaining his usual mask, solemnly agreed to travel to the Middle East and hear all sides before reporting on what we already knew: that the singed Clark would never move the embassy and that next time, with luck (there wasn't any), he would put his brain in gear before opening his mouth.

Stanfield of Arabia, pictured by the cartoonists on a camel, his humps and lumps melding in with his beast, dutifully trekked off to the outlandish outposts where his six-piece blue serge reminded all present of someone who had gotten lost on the way to lunch at the Pall Mall club. He was told, so the chagrined Clark flacks announced it, to take a year to do the study that any six-year-old could have done in ten minutes.

Stanfield had intended to spend his summer tending his new backyard asparagus crop in toney Rockcliffe Park, the lofty Ottawa enclave where snivel servants go to die. External affairs minister Flora MacDonald, flourishing the religious calendar issued to all new ministers in that portfolio (along with a guide on which fork to use), warned him not to go to the Middle East until Ramadan, the Moslem holy month, had passed, or until the Jewish holidays that follow were over.

Poor Stanfield. Visions of Thanksgiving appeared, then Hannukah, Christmas, New Year's, Passover, Easter and possibly April Fool's Day — just about the time the next year's asparagus crop would be demanding some fertilizer of its own. Wisely, he did a quick tour, allowing for a discreet interval before announcing the obvious: Joe Was had spent too long in High River devouring Robert's Rules of Order and not enough time examining the world atlas. The embassy was safe in Tel Aviv, and Stanfield, no doubt recalling his assessment of Clark as too high strung for this trade, went back to test the whiteness of the Rockcliffe asparagus.

Robert Lorne Stanfield (his staff always referred to him among themselves as "RLS") was a decent man who came along at the wrong time. Senator Grattan O'Leary, who has since gone to that great talkative, bibulous Ould Green Sod in the sky, called him "the most liberal, humane, and civilized mind on our political landscape."

In a magazine profile, John Aitken wrote of the 1972 Stanfield that he was

> in many ways a more interesting politician than Trudeau. He bristles with paradox. He invokes trust in an age that prefers excitement and acceleration. He is humble and we consider humility to be embarrassing. He is diffident and that quality, in this political decade, is catastrophic. . . . Stanfield has failed the public, simply by being what he is — an insuperably

reticent man who holds an office in which reticence is no virtue.

Says a former Ottawa staffer: "I never really had the feeling that RLS knew why he was there or what he was doing."

The Tories, as through their history, could never really get in sync with the times. They selected a dour patrician, who liked to walk to work, from an old-fashioned province with old-fashioned manners — just in time to go up against a dashing bachelor who drove a Mercedes-Benz and stood on his head at parties: the Model-T going up against the sports car. The party goes against the flow.

He was picked as leader in 1967 as something new, clobbered in 1968 while being revealed as something old, and the party was then stuck with him, because of his essential decency. No Brutus could assault this one. A private man, he had no business being exposed head on to the meat market of media politics. He was a bug out of water, a man from the most reticent part of the country pushed forward by the advertising masters of Toronto into the merciless maw of telegenic modern politics — where teeth and hair mean most.

Late one evening I was waiting for an MP outside the west door of the Commons. Stanfield appeared out the darkness in his white raincoat, the hunched figure, as always, appearing shorter than it should be. There was a full moon and we talked while MPs hurried home. We talked and talked and one got the impression he would have stayed there for hours. No hurry. No sweat. He had already announced he was leaving as leader and was patiently waiting for the leave-taking, no recriminations, no regrets, no complaints. Just a nice man on a nice night who enjoyed talking.

Clark Gable died shortly after making a movie, *The Misfits*, which was written by the playwright Arthur Miller, whose wife, Marilyn Monroe, was the co-star. In a copy of the screenplay given to Gable, Miller wrote: "To the man who did not know how to hate."

That will do also as a political epitaph for Robert Stanfield, a gentleman in a ruffians' game.

50

5 The Scarecrow

"I don't mind my legs and arms and body being stuffed, because I cannot get hurt. If anyone treads on my toes or sticks a pin into me, it doesn't matter, for I can't feel it. But I do not want people to call me a fool, and if my head stays stuffed with straw instead of with brains. . . . how am I to know anything?"

"If you're given a lemon, you make lemonade." — Saskatchewan Premier Grant Devine, explaining why he was supporting Joe Clark in the 1983 leadership campaign.

The Progressive Conservative caucus — with wives and girlfriends, assorted mistresses and covivants, plus the invited press and party functionaries — had its 1982 Christmas party in the ornate confines of Room 200 in the West Block on Parliament Hill.

I was standing over a drink, exchanging lies with Val Sears of the Toronto *Star*, when Joe Clark joined us, mainly, one surmised, because of the recent uncommonly favourable pieces Sears had penned after following Clark on a solo swing through Western Canada. They seemed quite pleased with one another.

Clark was scheduled to lead the Christmas carols later in the evening, and Sears said, in his tone of Anglican High Church hauteur for which he is celebrated, "I trust you're going to sing 'O Come All Ye Faithful.' I hope so, because I've already filed my piece indicating that you did so." This, of course, was only a month before the Winnipeg leadership review trauma, and Clark's ability to rally his flock was in some question.

Somewhat to my astonishment, but eventually my resignation, Joe Clark, when the carol singing came, obliged scribe Sears by singing "O Come All Ye Faithful."

Therein lies the fatal weakness of Joe Clark: wanting to please, not his own man, able to be swayed, looking for the short advantage. A stronger man, a more resolute leader, would have nodded, then scratched out in his mind any thought of singing the requested song and moved on. Sears would never have dared make such a request to a Trudeau. Joe Clark was not a leader, but a supplicant wanting applause.

When he was elected leader in February 1976, he waited until the third day of the Commons sitting before entering the House. After a round of welcoming speeches, he chose to reply to a remark by Ed Broadbent, saying that the NDP leader's "problems of internal disunity may continue; ours, of course, are over."

It was a magnificent debut of the lack of judgement that followed Clark through his short nine months in power and — eventually — led him to the preposterous Winnipeg decision in 1983 that 66.9 per cent of party support was not enough and that he must arrange his own funeral.

The first day in the Commons after being elected prime minister in 1979, rising to the right of the Speaker for the first time, a nervous Clark called Trudeau "Prime Minister." He had already made worse errors. In pseudo-macho style, he refused to give even one of the Dief veterans a token minor cabinet role and thereby earned their enmity forever.

Clark, running a new government that desperately needed the urban vote, shut out of the inner cabinet David Crombie, who had only been the most popular mayor in the history of Toronto, the largest city in the country, and who now controlled the largest budget, health and welfare, in cabinet. He gave the responsibility for Toronto organization (that is, patronage) to a minor-league loyalist, Ron Atkey, rather than Crombie.

On June 11, 1983, asked if his man would go to Clark after the first ballot, an aide to Crombie — the least vindictive man in Canada — said, "He'd rather put a .45 in his mouth." As might have been expected, a hopelessly outgunned Crombie, with only 116 votes, did not drop out after the first ballot but stayed on, thus preserving John Crosbie for another crucial ballot — and then going to Crosbie, who went to Mulroney. Bad, bad judgement has long consequences.

Another Prairie boy, Otto Lang, a Rhodes Scholar who sat opposite Clark as Trudeau's justice minister and transport minister before being swallowed by the anti-Liberal taste of Western Canada, always said that Joe Clark could never give a rationale for being prime minister other than that he wanted the job.

There was a reason, at the time, for Lester Pearson's becoming prime minister. There certainly was a reason, given the mood of the nation, for John Diefenbaker's being acclaimed prime minister. There was, obvious to all in the heady post-Expo euphoria, a clear reason for Pierre Trudeau in 1968.

As Lang points out, Clark became leader — and then prime minister — by default. (Joe Clark was the last to come to prominence of the group with whom he attended university. The University of Alberta mock parliament of Clark's era also produced Liberal leader Jim Coutts, who still has Trudeau's ear; Grant Notley, now the Alberta NDP leader; Bob Clark and Ray Speaker, later Alberta's Social Credit leader and deputy; Jim Foster, later the Alberta attorney general; Lou Hyndman, heir-apparent to Premier Peter Lougheed; Peter Hyndman, later a B.C. Socred cabinet minister. Then came the lowly Clark. His late rise explains why the Coutts-inspired Grits in Ottawa regarded him with such contempt.)

Although in his first years as leader, Clark was an object of fun and derision to the press wits of the realm, his Gallup standing simply eased on up. The response of the public was a resigned and futile shrug. He inspired no real warmth or enthusiasm, but he became the sixteenth prime minister of Canada because the electorate could not bear the Liberals.

53

Awkwardness succeeded. It is the age of the anti-hero. Woody Allen crossed with Jerry Ford stumbled toward the peak.

Blair Williams, a Montreal professor who was national director of the Liberal Party, has pointed out that politicians who lack a "place" outside politics do not tend to move with self-assurance, nor are likely to make sacrifices when it threatens their political vocation. "Too often they need the job, and because they need it they are captives, not leaders." Clark wanted the job "because it is his life; it is an essential part of his persona; it sustains him in society; he has nothing else to fall back on."

There is a wispy quality to Joe Clark. You try to take hold of the image, the personage, and he is elusive. There is nothing you can pin down, wrestle to earth, analyze, dissect, examine or massage. Joe Clark flits just out of reach; just about as puzzling and unknown as he was when he came from nowhere to assume the Tory crown from that other personality, Robert Lorne Stanfield.

Clark has a singular talent for circling around any specific subject, somewhat like a dog approaching a strange bush, so as to sniff out its exact centre and plumb it, explain it, smother and waffle it to death. His caution exhausts the listener until the audience falls, grateful, upon the slightest turgid conclusion, content at least in the knowledge that the chase is over.

He comes across as reasonable, polite, but roundabout, verbose, careful to block every possible semantic exit lest some errant thought escape into the void. It is a style understandable in a man who as a grade 11 student won a Rotary Club oratorical prize that sent him from High River to Ottawa just in time to witness John Diefenbaker in the triumph of the 1956 pipeline debate. To an eager high-school debator from Alberta, the rotund elaborations of the prophet from Prince Albert were an obvious influence.

It accounts for the curiously old-fashioned profundities of this forty-four-year-old who seems senile beyond his time. There are embellishments, flourishes, rococo clauses and ornamental bit-ends until the listener feels in need of a Black and Decker buzz saw to attack a Hampton Court maze of verbiage in vain search for a few nuggets of sense.

His elaborate, antiquated speaking manner and vocabulary perhaps are a guise to cover his physical awkwardness. He is an uncoordinated mechano doll out of some child's play kit, arms in no synchronization with the body, the long fingers of a Van Cliburn incessantly twitching, flexing, rubbing the lips, searching for some unseen solace. Those long spindly hands flit about nervously, pressing one another, flying to the pockets, fitfully tapping the table or whatever is available. One always suspected his aides wished he would take up smoking, just as René Lévesque's supporters try to hide his habit.

Clark is left-handed, each movement at the head table emphasizing how much out of rhythm he is with the physical world where others can jump mud puddles, tie reef knots, swim and stroll with ease. Everything seems out of sync when he walks, his arms swinging to the beat of a different drummer, the wrists and hands only vaguely connected to them. He is one of those rare people who does not appear *comfortable* walking. You want to shove a chair at him to put him out of his agony.

All this physical awkwardness has nothing to do with the ability to govern, but it obviously affected his ability to attract the voters — and to reassure the troubled Tory delegates who began their agonizing reappraisals almost on the day they anointed him. Mackenzie King could never have ruled in the age of television.

Clark never really appears at ease in public; once he senses the cameras are on him, he freezes even more and tends to bump into things, like bayonets. A Jerry Ford image, once acquired in the press public/mind, is a difficult albatross to shake.

He is defensive about his failures in life. At the Winnipeg gathering in January 1983 he appeared truly rattled when a youth delegate heckler shouted, "Can you do it for real, Joe?"

55

Clark shot back: "What have you done for real? I once won the office of prime minister." The youth came back: "I got through law school." Clark snapped that "Possession of a law degree doesn't mean you possess any good judgement, uh, necessarily."

Beside him, the face of his wife was frozen in a nervous grin. Maureen McTeer graduated as a lawyer, but doesn't practice.

Clark, on another occasion, showed his wry side when he said, "I wanted to be a lawyer, until I married one."

There are, if you must know, three Joe Clarks. The public was never allowed to discover it, but there are three thin men thrashing around inside that elongated blue suit, tripping over one another, bumping into opposing personae, jealously fighting for a bigger piece of the action. The man who was briefly prime minister of Canada, the hiccup of history, is a house divided unto itself, a schizophrenic mélange, an intellectual scrambled egg.

There is, first of all, the Joe Clark called Bravado. This is the Joe Clark who defiantly announces, at a press conference within twenty-four hours of taking office, that of course he will be moving the Canadian embassy in Israel from Tel Aviv to Jerusalem, and that he is serving notice to the civil service and diplomats that he didn't need their advice, and so there, take that.

He could read. He knew that Larry Zolf had dubbed him the Man from Insipid. He knew that the press that trailed him on his world tour (celebrated in song, skit and anecdotes that last to dawn) regarded his conduct in foreign climes as gauche and embarrassing. The Jerusalem ploy was the answer to the taunts: he would make a bold foreign initiative, a slap in the face to those who claimed he was lost in the world beyond High River.

This was the Joe Clark from Bravado, a man who was later made to pay the price, despatching Stanfield to become the battered bean bag of the Middle East. It's one form of his personality that bursts forth, then retreats, rather regretful that it was allowed out of the tent.

56

Bravado, naturally, requires that the owner demonstrate a certain amount of overkill. It should be remembered, therefore, before we leave this portion of the scrambled ego, that while at university Joe Clark met regularly with a group of pals for those usual college bantering and whither-the-world sessions. It was Joe's habit to arrive each time with a new word that none of the others had ever heard of. Another small clue to his personality. (Fans of the tortured English language will understand, therefore, the man's liking for such atrocities as "privatization" and "specificity.")

Just as Pierre Trudeau in his youth was a brilliant loner, Joe Clark was an industrious busybody. There was the time he came home from school telling his mother he had the choice of six essay topics. He sat down and did all six. In 1957, there was Osgoode Hall law student Ted Rogers — now the Toronto cable TV king — as leader of the Tory student federation. On a trip to Edmonton, he mentioned to a freshman named Clark the need for a national campaign pamphlet for students. A week later Clark had a draft on Rogers' Toronto desk — so meticulous that it went untouched to press and ten thousand copies went to campuses across the land.

There was the weekend he came home from university and, aflame with youthful political passion, got on the phone to his Tory contacts around the country. When his parents eventually got the bill, it amounted to $185. They quietly paid it, their bow to the awkward boy who wasn't outstanding, flubbed law school and never seemed to have attracted a single girl until he married his researcher, Maureen McTeer.

The second Joe Clark, fighting the first, is the Joe Clark from Cautious. This man really is a conservative; he likes to make haste slowly (interrupted only by those aberrant bursts of bravado to prove that he is not cautious).

It was the Clark from Cautious who immediately after he became PM task-forced the country to death. Of course we're going to junk Petrocan was the campaign pledge and the post-election assertion. But wait. First, a task force, composed of raging capitalists from the private sector and including no member representing the public, should investigate the possibility and be stuck with the responsibility for privatization, if necessary, but not necessarily privatization.

Poor Stanfield is to investigate Jerusalem in hopes that it will go away. Mortgage interest deductibility? Well, we're sticking by the pledge but we just haven't decided all the details about a project that will help those who don't need help and hurt those who do.

The cautious Joe Clark put Lowell Murray into the Senate as a way of correcting a mistake made by the Joe Clark from Bravado—the appointment to the same chamber of the brash Robert de Cotret. Since it became apparent that de Cotret was in danger of being eaten for breakfast by the long-slumbering Liberal economic cadre in the upper house, the calm Murray was the life preserver for the callow and impetuous de Cotret. Caution always follows bravado, an instinct that marked Clark's whole life in politics.

The first one hundred days of his 1979 government? Journalism reverberated with comparisons to the first days of Kennedy and Pearson, not to mention Roosevelt. The cautious Joe Clark, from a cautious small town, instead shut down the country, cooling its temperature, adjusting it to his cautious style, refusing the entreaties to call Parliament.

In response to the red-fanged cries of Conservatives across the land, demanding an instant blood-letting among the bloated Liberal patronage appointments, Clark hummed and waited. The fashionable bars of the Dominion were awash with the obscenities of young Tory lawyers awaiting their chance to dip their blue noses into the trough so long reserved for their Grit drinking companions. Caution prevailed — until it was too late.

Intruding on those two warring elements within the same bosom is the most secret Joe Clark, the private one. Clark is, like Stanfield, an entirely different person when relaxed. Public appearances, rather than bringing out the shine of a Trudeau or a Kennedy (a Howard Pawley?), seem to mystify and perplex Clark, rendering him even more a wind-up man and eliciting the arch chuckle that echoes in the rain barrel of insincerity.

58

In private, when he trusts himself to lower his guard (Clark has a sense of wariness toward the press of an ex-junior reporter who didn't quite make it), he has a nice dry wit that verges on old-press-club cynicism. In public, he is stiff. Trudeau, so casual and slanging in public, is hard to break through to — if not impossible — in private sessions, and his sense of humour is meagre.

One night, on a campaign jet, I went forward from the raucous press cattle-car section in the rear (the Francophone reporters, as always, standing in song, in great spirits; the Anglophone segment, as always, seated, drinking and bitching) to chat with Clark, he clad in his yellow cardigan that we called his Perry Como sweater, no one having seen such a specimen for years.

We sat and nattered and I asked him whether the incessant Parliament Hill denigration of his supposed defects did not get to him. Weren't there some days, I said, when he looked in the shaving mirror in the morning and wondered whether it was all worthwhile?

"Sure," he said. "It hurt. A lot of it hurt."

He looked at me, evenly, honestly but without rancour. "Some of the things you've written have hurt. Don't kid yourself." He's a remarkably self-composed man in private — which no one in public would ever guess.

We saw intermittent, jerky evidence of the first two Clarks, but little if any of the latter. He knew vaguely where he wanted to go. He was just slightly confused about how to get there — and which one of him was going.

The result of all this was that the Tories got not a leader but an organizer — carefully stage-managed for seven painful years in an artful disguise and passed off as leader. To improve his television manner, the handlers sent him to a Toronto hair stylist who determined he had been parting his hair on the wrong side all his life. Brilliant politics! The party tried to make him, like Stanfield, into something he never was. In the *Wizard of Oz*, the farmer says, "This fellow will scare the crows fast enough. He looks just like a man."

This newspaperman always watched Joe Clark with

59

puzzlement. Did he get any *fun* out of life? He once said, "I've spent fifteen years of my life in meetings." Therein may lie the problem. You don't learn about life in meetings.

Don Macdonald once ruled himself out of an earlier Liberal leadership sweepstakes because, he claimed, he didn't have "the royal jelly." Did Joe Clark ever really have the royal jelly? Or was it force-fed into his carcass by those around him who saw the prize so close and yet so fragile, so obtainable yet so susceptible? He may have been done in by those around him whose personal goals surpassed his own gifts. Ambition without talent is a terrible thing.

6 Off to See the Wizard

*"The road is straight to the South . . . but it is said
to be full of dangers to travellers. There are wild beasts
in the woods, and a race of queer men who do not
like strangers to cross their country.*

*"As for the Scarecrow, having no brains, he
walked straight ahead, and so stepped into holes and
fell at full length on the hard bricks. It didn't hurt
him, however, and Dorothy would pick him up and
set him upon his feet again."*

There is a flourishing little cottage industry in Ottawa. It is
based on Joe Clark's famous around-the-world-in-80-daze tour
of 1979. The lesser part of the industry is composed of the
few journalists who were actually on the trip—and who meet
for a commemorative lunch each January 18 (the one who
first exhausts his stone of memorable Clark travel quotes
must pick up the bill).

The larger part of the industry is made up of an amazing
number of people who have become great experts on the tour,
not hampered at all by the fact that they missed the trip. One
columnist for a terribly serious Toronto paper has appointed
himself an absolute authority on the subject and, in his defence of Clark, has created a new myth: the myth that Clark
was an innocent on the trip and the image he manufactured
for himself was somehow all someone else's creation.

It is about time that someone who actually was aboard
that ill-fated starship, meaning Dr. Foth, did a little autopsy
and a little explaining.

I am aided by a non-participant who *has* become the world
expert on the tour. He is a bright and industrious young man
by the name of Chris Staples, a Carleton University student
who, for his honours research project for Journalism 498, had

the ingenious idea of investigating the controversial press coverage of the world tour. He interviewed everyone — all the reporters, all of Clark's staff, the travel agents who choreographed the disaster, even the soldier who held the bayonet that Clark, in his ambulatory adventures, had so much trouble with. He has produced a thick tome, an excellent piece of work. His thesis is entitled *Lost Bags and Bayonets* and is a very entertaining and informative work.

There are those who think that what emerged from that tour cost Joe Clark a majority government in the election that came four months later in 1979 — a majority that would have allowed John Crosbie's "bood-jet" (budget) to pass unimpeded and would have allowed Clark to continue as prime minister who-knows-for-how-long rather than becoming, as now, a footnote in the history books.

At the time the world tour was announced, your blushing agent had been predicting — and urging — for some time, in newspaper and magazine columns, on radio and TV, soapboxes and wherever else I could find a trapped listener, that Clark would and should be the next prime minister. The sated twits who drove the stale Liberal machine obviously needed a spell in Opposition to cleanse themselves.

My publisher at the time, Clark Davey of the Vancouver *Sun*, was of the Conservative persuasion and agreed that observing Clark at first hand on a world tour would be a good test of whether a prime-minister-to-be could stand up to the pressures and scrutiny of a full election campaign. The idea came from Ted Bolwell, one of the finest newspapermen in the country, who was editorial director of the FP chain of papers which then owned the *Sun*. The paper was strike-bound but Bolwell assigned me to file despatches to all the FP papers, stretching from Montreal to Victoria.

The first inclination of the boy-scout nature of what was to follow came when I received the itinerary mailed by the Clark office in December 1978. It indicated that they couldn't spell ("embasy," "sittuated," "specailty") and were obviously unfamiliar with Italy's state airline — "Ali-talia." Maureen McTeer was a spouse and "lawyers"; Jeffrey Lyons was a Toronto "lawyer"; Canadian Press, the best-known news organization in the country, was "Canadian News."

More incredible was the schedule that was Mission Impossible at a mere glance. The Clarkians had planned only a fourteen-hour connection between Japan and India — (Tokyo to Manila to Bangkok to New Delhi) that hinged on a sixty-five-minute change of airlines in Bangkok. Sixty-five minutes to move two dozen bodies, thirty-six pieces of baggage, TV equipment and assorted flotsam and jetsam? This was the future government? I smacked my furrowed forehead in amazement.

The 1979 world tour was the brainchild, ironically enough, of Doug Roche, the sensitive, thoughtful Edmonton MP who is an internationalist, a far cut above the standard slash-and-bluster Prairie Tories who flail away at pillows from the Tory backbench during Question Period. After a 1978 trip to Asia and the Middle East, Roche, as Clark's external affairs critic, recommended that the inexperienced Clark embark on an extensive international "fact-finding" trip, including Jordan as a "window" into Middle East problems, and India as a leader of the Third World. It was, as Chris Staples puts it, "another chapter in the education of Joe Clark."

In June 1976 Clark had visited Washington on his first foreign trip as leader. "The ambassador to the United States," recalls senior advisor Jim Gillies, "threw a fancy luncheon at the Jockey Club and it was quite clear that it was all strange for Joe." This trip was followed that fall by a seventeen-day tour of six European capitals.

The logistics were "a disaster," remembers Doug Small, the effervescent chief of Global TV's Ottawa bureau, who covered the European tour for Canadian Press. Reporters, sympathetic to the greenness of the new young leader, were often left carrying the luggage of Clark and aide Ian Green. Green was the advance man for the European tour — and the world trip three years later.

Ian Green was a long drink of water, with a fey smile, a young man who gave the appearance of being the second juvenile lead in a Noel Coward play. He was well-bred, polite, but condescending, always giving the impression that he was slightly above this band of fumbling opportunists who had come into fortune through a lottery, rather than true inheritance.

The idea for the world tour was to present Clark—luxuriating in ten October 1978 by-election victories and a ten-point lead in the Gallup—as a competent world statesman, since Canada obviously viewed him as the PM-to-be. Tory pollster Allan Gregg, he of the mixmaster hair, says the tour's original purpose, to educate Joe Clark, became secondary to an image-making goal. "It was a beauty contest. They were there to have their pictures taken. Anyone who says differently, I think, is lying."

Bob Lewis, now managing editor of *Maclean's*, remembers how at pre-tour briefings Clark's chief-of-staff Bill Neville made a "big deal" of the fact they had the prime ministers of Japan and India lined up to meet Canada's next prime minister. Small recalls, "It was pompous beyond belief."

Ian Green, now disappeared into the safety of a government job, says, "We knew full well there was no substance to the trip. We finally decided that we couldn't keep the press from coming. We'd take the risk and hope for the best."

The Boy Amateurs, their eyes aglow with perceived power, set off into the ozone, fifty-three thousand miles and five countries in twelve days before them. The Ottawa *Citizen*, in an editorial three days previous, warned:

> The risk for Clark, hardly a seasoned traveller, is not in dealing with strange customs in foreign lands but with the attention of the Canadian press corps traveling with him. . . . There will be days when the press, intent on filing a report-a-day whether Canada needs it or not, will be picking the lint out of Clark's belly button to prove to their bosses that this is just not a junket. . . . He'll have to take the bad with the good, and it's an even bet that we'll be hearing and reading some nit-picking criticisms before he returns to Canada on January 18.

Nit-picking? At least four of us, charitable to the core, tried to warn the cocky Clarkians about the obvious ambush waiting on the goofy connection between Tokyo and New Delhi. In the lounge at Dorval airport in Montreal, before taking off, Don Sellar of Southam News tried unsuccessfully to convince Donald Doyle, Clark's press secretary, that the sixty-five-minute connection was too tight. (Air Canada, as with all IATA members, won't book passengers through Toronto airport on an hour's connection, since they can't guarantee luggage transfer in that time.)

Someone said to Doyle, "If you get our bags through Bangkok you will not buy another drink around the world." Doyle said not to worry. There was an element of super-confidence.

Donald Doyle, his eyes forever shaded behind smoked glasses, was a man in search of a rationale for his role, never being able to shield the fact he was a one-time newspaperman now trying to con working reporters. His embarrassed grin was a working weapon. He always exuded the feeling that he knew what he was doing was not entirely respectable.

Clark had been shipped ahead for a week's holiday in Hawaii to ensure that he was rested and calm for the adventure ahead. "My image needs no building," he said rather loftily on arriving in Tokyo. "I'm not going to win the election abroad."

What was the purpose of this trip? "It's useful to have been somewhere."

Clark has an archness, a self-mocking sense of humour that is quite subtle — when seen in private. He has never realized — or had never then — that when written down in black-and-white print it doesn't translate, and comes across as sounding, well, dumb.

The well-rested future prime minister, on his first morning in Tokyo, toured a park with Canadian Ambassador Bruce Rankin — strictly a fake photo opportunity for the TV cameras. Gazing at flowers, Clark turned to Rankin and asked, "What season is it?"

It was January. Japan is well into the northern hemisphere. Rankin, a raw-boned millionaire who looks like a cross between John Wayne and Jack Horner and talks with the bluntness of both, turned and looked at the future PM with the look one gives a six-year-old who has just spilled jello on your best rug.

"Winter," said Ambassador Rankin to Mr. Clark.

(Three days later, on arrival in India, Clark asked a guide what season it was. It was still January. The guide, with a look in his eyes somewhat similar to that of Ambassador Rankin, said, politely, "It's winter." Carol McIvor, a serious CBC radio reporter, felt that Clark's ignorance of geography was such that he actually believed we had crossed the equator and would therefore be in summer. There is no way of proving that of course, but I had — from his sense of discombobulation and unease — the same feeling.)

There was Clark explaining, after his first meeting with the Japanese, that "translators tend to slow the conversation" — an amazing discovery delivered with the seriousness of someone who had just stumbled upon the invention of the wheel. Speaking through an interpreter, he found, was "a little bit like an arthritic ballet."

Aides would shuffle nervously, and reporters, on hearing lines like this, would look sideways at one another, puzzling silently over the prospect that here was our future prime minister missing a beautiful opportunity to keep his mouth shut.

Dr. Foth, beginning to grow twitchy over his prediction of deserved death for the Grit regime, filed a piece that led off: "Has Joe Clark discovered his own round-the-world football?" It went on: "The lack of experience in the Clark entourage will be put to its greatest test in Clark's departure today. His office has somehow made travel arrangements via Egypt Air that go via Manila before a scheduled one-hour transfer in Bangkok on the way to New Delhi, a journey that will take fourteen hours. When asked who booked the flight, some astute Japanese observers offer that it could be only Prime Minister Trudeau."

The innocents abroad could not be deterred. Egypt Air, known fondly in the territory as "Terror Air," had a well-known reputation — well known, that is, to everyone but Ottawa's Voyageur Travel, the Tory travel agents, who seemed to be familiar only with an airline schedule. Staff at Rankin's embassy tried to persuade the Clarkians to make other arrangements, futilely. This was, after all, a future PM ascendant.

The Foreign Correspondents Club of Tokyo made such a convincing argument about Terror Air's unreliability and poor safety record that two of the journalists accompanying Clark, fearing for their loved ones, attempted to book alternate flights to Delhi. Dr. Foth, as the den father of the troupe, eventually convinced them to stay on the theory that if the future PM was to die in a plane crash into the South China Sea, they owed it to themselves to be there to report it. The logic finally sunk in. Always stick with the story.

Terror Air proved to be as good as advertised. The Boeing 707 was scheduled to leave Tokyo on Wednesday, January 9, at 1500 hours, make a brief stopover at Manila in the Philippines before proceeding to Thailand, arriving at 2140 hours. In Bangkok, the delegation was to board a Lufthansa flight to New Delhi, arriving at 0120 hours. A meeting with Prime Minister Desai was scheduled for 1500 hours that same day.

Late taking off, of course, Terror Air 707 did a number of quick correcting manoeuvres over a choppy Tokyo Bay that reminded one for all the world of O.J. Simpson dodging through an airline terminal.

"The structure was groaning," says Norm Fetterley, Ottawa man for Toronto television's CFTO. "We were jammed in like sardines. Up until then I had enjoyed flying terrifically. I have never been comfortable in an airplane since. For about two years after that I was scared stiff even to fly to Toronto."

Carol McIvor says, "I was sitting in a seat that had bloodstains all over the back of it and two holes. I don't know whether they were bullet holes or not. There was no alcohol. If there was any time in my life that I needed a drink, it was going on that flight."

The dicey drama took on a touch of high farce in Manila. As the Clark forces nervously checked their watches, the flight was boarded by some fifty Filipino dockworkers in overalls headed for the Red Sea port of Jeddah, Saudi Arabia. "Crammed to the rafters," wrote Southam's Don Sellar, "devoid of air conditioning and out of Scotch whisky in minutes, this was a plane to remember. After a few hours it smelled like a camel drivers' convention."

In Bangkok, the desperate Canadian ambassador had used diplomatic clout to persuade Lufthansa to keep their Delhi-bound flight waiting on the tarmac. Shaken, dehydrated and casting glances askance at the white-faced staff of the future PM, we sprinted through the darkness into a Lufthansa 747 — clean, cool and politely staffed, a new world. The waiting passengers, a trifle impatient, studied the incoming rush of frantic, rumpled, embarrassed and angry transients — who had already been in the air seven hours — no doubt taking us for a clutch of misdirected tourists who had won some radio contest. Little did they know that they were gazing upon a future prime minister and his entourage.

Left behind in the Bangkok confusion (along with Clark's dignity and the credibility of his logistical planners) was all the luggage, and, hilariously, most of the equipment of the two television crews who were along to record what was essentially a world-wide photo opportunity. It was a beauty contest and someone had misplaced the judges.

The Boy Amateurs apparently had never thought of such a thing as a standby overnight kit for their leader. In Delhi, toothpaste and razors were hustled with help from the Canadian High Commission, and Clark arrived for a state dinner with Prime Minister Desai in the tired suit that had endured the flight connecting four countries.

By then, it had become clear we were dealing with neophytes who shouldn't have been allowed outside without the strings tied securely to their mittens. Dapperly dressed in white shoes and an electric-blue leisure suit, chief-of-staff Neville, who was technically going to be the second most powerful man in Canada if and when Clark became PM, stepped gingerly through a dung-filled Indian village, snapping all the colourful poverty with his camera. It was straight out of the Elks hall.

Clark lapsed into his stunning collection of inanities: "What is the totality of his land?" to an interpreter on a farm; "How old are the chickens?" "You are not anticipating a significant cereal production?" to a guide in an impoverished area. To doomed women in a dismal village: "I very much appreciate the very cordial greeting."

There was a mad last-minute scramble to make sure everyone got on board the late-night Alitalia flight to the next stop, Athens, a certain journalist having to bully all the press luggage through customs when it became clear the Clarkians had frayed around the edges and were coming apart. For some strange reason, which has never been explained to this day, advance man Ian Green failed to advance on to Athens as the itinerary advertised and, tight-lipped, managed with some suspense to garner a seat on the overbooked flight.

By this time, the Clark handlers, sensing the reporters on the "fact-finding" tour were finding out too many facts about their charge, decided to hide Clark even more completely from media scrutiny.

We actually were quite a compact group, a group that Clark could have gotten to know easily since there was little of substance happening. While the media group numbered fourteen, only six were of the pencil press (Lewis from *Maclean's*, Small from CP, Jeff Simpson of the *Globe and Mail*, Steve Handelman of the Toronto *Star*, Sellar of Southam News and the ever-vigilant Dr. Foth) — the others were radio types or TV men, with their trailing umbilical life-support systems. But instead of telling us about his hopes and dreams, Clark remained hidden away in his hotel suite each night, while his paranoid aides read despatches from home.

Actually, the man who killed Clark (or, more accurately, allowed him to kill himself) was the most inexperienced reporter on the tour. His name was Brian Kennedy, a radio reporter out of Broadcast News in the Victoria press gallery. Broadcast News brass, in a move whose logic paralyzed me, sent on the tour not a veteran from the Ottawa press gallery but Kennedy, because he was from Victoria. Sending him around the world would be "cheaper," they thought, since Victoria was closer to Japan, the first stop, than Ottawa. Since the earth is round, and Kennedy would eventually have to return to his base, this accounting dazzled me. But I digress.

Knowing he had never been anywhere, and was up against Ottawa pros, the young and brash Kennedy stuck to Clark like a burr, wearing him like a second vest. His prying mike, attached to the creepy-peepy on his back, lurked just a malaprop away. At every stop, Kennedy would dash away to a convenient phone to send out over the underwater cables one of those illuminating thirty-second clips on another Clark goof that would speckle the newscasts all day on the fifty Broadcast News outlets across the country.

Kennedy, who soon came to regard Clark as the mother lode of non-sequiturs, dogged the future prime minister like a living child. It was Kennedy who surreptitiously stood behind Clark, mike aready, when the future PM was shown, in the foyer of the Knesset, Israel's parliament, the world-famous tapestries by Marc Chagall that depict the turmoil of the Jewish people from Moses to the Holocaust. Joe Clark had one all-purpose answer for every stunning sight he saw on his odyssey around the world. It was: "I see."

While a pretty young guide movingly and eloquently explained the meaning and significance of the sixty-six-foot-long art work, what it meant to her people, Joe Clark said "I see" twenty-one times.

The problem is that Joe Clark really is a nice guy. He is kind, he is considerate. He would never do anything intentionally rude. He is, in a way, a sort of sociological freak, a mutation from the 1930s. Watching him carefully at close range over an extended period of time, one gets the impression of Cecil Trueheart, the second lead in a Noel Coward play set in the landed gentry belt of Kent.

Clark himself even knows the reason why. High River, Alberta, despite its Gary Cooperish name, was one of those Prairie towns populated in early days by remittance men —

70

the semi-failed heirs of the English gentility, sent abroad to lose themselves so as not to disgrace the family name.

In High River, of all places, they played *cricket*. A polo team from High River actually won the 1912 world championship. As he explains, it was a town where manners meant something. It wasn't Gary Cooper at all. It was Noel Coward, within sight of the Rockies.

Watching Joe Clark day in, day out, night in, night out, as he circled the globe on an indoctrination tour that may have been the worst political decision since Suez, one was reminded constantly of that self-description of his background. It was the vicar's tea party across four continents, a continual "thank-you-very-very-much" while stepping backward for fear of giving offense.

Thank-you-very-very-much was the catchword of the tour. Within days, after hearing it incessantly directed at prime ministers, subway attendants, minor officialdom and any potted palm that twitched, the Clark entourage mocked it, imitated it, repeated it, set it into iambic pentameter and Gilbert and Sullivan rhymes. "Thank-you-very-very-much" and "I see" became the metaphors of a future prime minister's introduction to the world.

Herein lies the tragedy of Joe Clark, a decent and polite man, now middle-aged, who is courageous and left the leadership he should never have attempted with such dignity and magnanimity. At the age of thirty-nine, he had the opportunity to visit five of the oldest and most interesting nations on earth: Japan, India, Greece, Israel, Jordan.

Watching him at close-hand, I saw a man who not only had no knowledge of history, art, culture, cuisine, theatre or religion, but who had no *interest* in those areas.

Even supposedly cynical journalists, marching off the exact route that Christ was made to carry the cross and seeing the exact spot where he was crucified, were moved by their Sunday school memories. Our future PM appeared bored; or perhaps, more accurately, distracted.

The further the tour advanced, the more Clark seemed glazed over by it all. It was as if he could not absorb it. He

71

seemed to want out of it. Perhaps aware that he was out of his depth, he didn't appreciate the prying press also being aware of that fact.

What I saw was a one-dimensional man, uneasy and uninterested in the world outside the cosy political structure. (Voters eventually detected the same.) My whole view of Clark has been shaped by that experience. Nothing that has happened under his purview since then has surprised me.

The most experienced reporter on the tour, in fact, was Rae Corelli, the grizzled Toronto *Star* veteran who had long been that paper's legal correspondent and was in 1979 a commentator and host on Global TV (he now has a CBC show in Vancouver). Corelli, a taciturn sort, kept to himself and said little in the early days of the tour, not believing what he was seeing.

He then aired one piece that began: "Phileas Fogg went around the world in 80 days in a balloon filled with hot air. Joe Clark has managed the same feat in 10 days — minus the balloon." Another broadcast started: "The Conservative Party of Canada has spent more than $30,000 so Joe Clark could learn about the world. Unfortunately, the world has learned about Joe Clark."

The Rover Boys Abroad grew in number to twenty-seven with the arrival, in Israel, of Maureen McTeer, two prominent Tory fundraisers with their wives, a Conservative Party photographer and two politicians. Robert Parker, the Tory MP for Eglinton, and Ron Atkey, the deposed MP from St. Paul's, had ridings that encompassed the largest portion of Toronto's Jewish voters. They had urged Clark to include Israel in his tour because they hoped it would help them get elected. The Tory photographer was along for that purpose.

Irving Gerstein, head of People's Jewellers, and lawyer Jeffrey Lyons both were long-time friends of Clark and important fundraisers in the Toronto Jewish community. It was this foursome that suggested to their green leader the supposed vote-getting pledge to move the Canadian embassy from Tel Aviv to Jerusalem. (For their troubles, neither Parker or Atkey survived the 1980 election.)

Atkey and Parker, arriving from Canada with tales of horror from the tour in the daily headlines, could not believe that Clark's handlers — the future government of Canada — would not allow him to put his feet up with the press.

At the meeting with Prime Minister Menachem Begin, the Israeli PM entered the room with a puzzled expression, not able momentarily, to pick out the future Canadian leader from his entourage. Clark, as Dalton Camp puts it, "has a small magnetic field."

At a meeting with Opposition leader Shimon Peres, Clark appeared startled, then unhappy, then uncomfortable and unsure of himself when Peres waved away the Clark aides, who were herding out the press after the usual phoney "photo opportunity," and invited the scribblers to sit down and listen.

Sellars, in a news analysis piece, called the session "one of the more illuminating sights seen in Canadian politics in several years." The meeting was "not a satisfying portrait of a future Canadian prime minister in action."

Student Staples, conducting the autopsy, found the Peres session significant, the first one of the tour that was open to the media. "The Peres meeting made us suspicious of Clark's other private meetings," said Doug Small. "We wondered if Clark was always this unsure of himself."

Clark's twitchiness of tongue and body was contrasted by the appearance of Maureen McTeer, genuinely pretty, now stylish, relaxed and pleasant, chattering away in French to a Canadian soldier, possessing just the right touch of light banter needed for these stiff occasions. Her presence merely emphasized the stick-man image of her uneasy husband, a creature — a *victim!* — of the parliamentary system, painfully unsure of himself once outside the formal structure of the high-school-debating atmosphere.

The Golan Heights, the strategic high ground controlling Israel's eastern border with Syria, rise steeply out of the dusky desert. It was here at Camp Zouani, a lonely, desolate outpost that was home for 125 Canadian soldiers who acted as a buffer between Israeli and Syrian forces, that Joe Clark was to review a small honour guard.

There were seven soldiers, bayonets tipping their rifles at head-height in the first row. There were five in the back row. Joe Clark, stiff as always when spectators and cameras are watching, moved past the first five soldiers and then — for some reason one knows not — attempted a brisk left turn to review the second row.

There was only one problem. Soldiers Six and Seven were still there in the front row. A perturbed Master Corporal Ken Metke of Comox, B.C. was Six. "I could sense what he was going to do," Metke told Doug Small, "but I wasn't about to move."

Jeff Simpson and Dr. Foth, trailing the action about a yard away, looked at one another in horror and moaned. The tour that had started out Keystone Kops was turning into Buster Keaton.

Clark bumped into Metke's right side, just missing the upright bayonet, whirled, did a corrective action somewhat like Egypt Air's and finally safely rounded Soldiers Six and Seven before attempting the arduous journey down the second row of the honour guard — which by now was more twitchy, understandably, than the uncoordinated and unhappy Tory leader.

An embarrassed Clark explained later that he had "never inspected an honour guard before," an affliction that encompasses most of the human race. "I'm sorry. I apologize. I should have stayed in line." Do future prime ministers apologize? Should they?

Ken Metke, now a sergeant, lives in Penhold, Alberta. He remembers. "Mr. Clark had his head down while he was walking. I guess he just turned too soon."

Doug Small filed a story on the CP wire, stating that Clark, while inspecting a guard of honour, had "collided with a Canadian soldier and nearly cut his head on a rifle bayonet." Which was true, since the rifles protruded at the required fifteen-degree angle. But the situation was not helped by some excited CP rewrite man who translated this into a lead that ran in several papers, explaining that "Opposition Leader Joe Clark almost had his head cut off on a rifle bayonet yesterday while inspecting a 12-man guard of honour on the lonely Golan Heights."

The inclusion of the ludicrous "off" in the copy, whether accidental or not, understandably enraged the confused and tired Clarkians, who by now were aware of the horrendous press coverage the Rover Boys were getting back home. Small also reported that Joe had then been smacked by a door leading into the camp mess, as Atkey walked behind him, mocking him for the press' benefit. After Clark visited the sick bay on the Golan Heights, Atkey smirked to reporters, "Watch out. He walked into the needle."

Soldiers in the camp store later presented him with a colourful tapestry of an Egyptian harem. "It's as close as I'll ever get to one," said Joe. "You're damn right," said Mo, who was right behind him. And so it went.

Clark's caravan of private cars and press bus left Jerusalem, delayed all the way behind a large yellow garbage truck, and crossed the River Jordan — a stream that would not even qualify as a creek in any self-respecting British Columbia hamlet.

By this time Clark seemed completely zonked by culture shock, a lust for the friendly attention of the assassins of the House of Commons clear in his eyes. Chief-of-Staff Neville, the shine gone from his white shoes, was seething with concealed rage. Press secretary Donald Doyle was as inscrutably incommunicative as usual. (Only the Tories, with their gifts, would decide to recruit a francophone as Clark's press secretary — a wise move — and then manage to find someone from Quebec whose given name and surname would indicate him to the public as an anglophone. Even their PR backfires.) Ian Green wasn't speaking to anyone, including airline clerks.

The amiable Sinclair Stevens, listed in the "notional itinerary" as "economic and finance policy coordinator, P.C. Party of Canada" — that is, babysitter — endured everything in silent bemusement, remembering only to press close to Clark's shoulder every time a TV camera or photographer came over the horizon.

In Jordan, Clark's seemingly unending fund of inanities were once again put into play. "This is a well," while standing before a well. "You have a lot of rocks here," to a guide in a rock-filled desolate sparse field.

In Amman, in an office chamber in King Hussein's palace, Clark stood stiffly, not saying a word, for forty minutes while waiting for the diminutive king to appear. Hussein, in not so subtle a fashion, was making his feelings known that the Tories had spent three days in Israel (in search of votes for two Toronto seats they eventually lost) and had scheduled only twenty-six hours in Jordan to hear the Arab side of the unending argument.

The next morning, before the Rover Boys flew home to Canada, in the middle of a restaurant in the Jordan Inter-Continental Hotel, Clark held a "working breakfast" press conference. The last day of the tour; the first and only press conference. (By this time I had been smacking my brow in amazement so often I developed migraines.)

I asked Clark, considering the obvious amateurish level of his aides' preparation for this trip, whether he was considering making any changes in his staff on the way to a prime ministership that seemed inevitable.

He replied, testily, that he had the finest staff available and was proud of them and would be sticking with them to the end. It was, not the first time, the example of an indecisive man attempting to prove he was decisive. (I mentioned to Doyle and Green later that they should ship me a cheque since, considering the man's comments on the record, they could never be fired and now had guaranteed employment tenure.)

Everything held true to form. On the final seventeen-hour ordeal back to Ottawa, the Royal Jordanian flight, delayed on the Amman runway, was further inconvenienced in New York due to snow. As the jet had approached New York, a friendly stewardess asked a discouraged and played-out Joe Clark whether he was flying in from Japan. Said Clark, "In a manner of speaking." The Rover Boys missed their connection to Toronto and on to Ottawa. Instead, they went by Eastern Airlines to Montreal's Dorval, arriving near midnight, and then taxied two hours to Ottawa in four hired Cadillac limousines. As an exhausted *Maclean's* bureau chief Bob Lewis fell into the arms of his wife in his Ottawa home, there came a knock at the door. It was the driver of the limo that had just delivered him. The car had broken down and he wanted to phone a cab.

The fallout from the junket of the Innocents Abroad was consequential. Bill Neville, he of the white shoes, feels today that the tour may have cost the Conservatives a majority government in 1979. "It gave our opponents a 'file of ridicule.' There's nothing more damaging than that." Clark himself feels the lost bags and bayonets translated into fewer votes: "I believe the coverage of the tour created several image perceptions which were a factor in our party's failure to attain a majority."

That's a revealing quote. Joe Clark's failure as a politician came about because he could not recognize reality, persisting in his fluke leadership even when he had lost public credibility and the trust of his caucus. (Clark told interrogator Staples: "Take that whole thing about the bayonet, for instance. Nothing happened there. I was reviewing the honour guard. It was just physically impossible. Nothing happened at all." Any man who believes that nothing happened is a man out of touch with reality, who prefers selective history to the truth.)

Actually, it was to an unknowing Ron Ziegler that Joe Clark owed his miserable fortunes on his non-news zip around the globe. It was Ziegler, the White House press secretary for Tricky Dicky Nixon, who invented that now-accepted charade called the "photo opportunity."

Ziegler was also the man who devised the hilarious non-word "misspoke." As in, "The President misspoke himself," meaning the President had either lied or goofed. It was in the fine Orwellian tradition of Newspeak (white is black, lies are truth), and so was the Nixonian introduction of the "photo opportunity."

It is childish simplicity, in its purpose. Since reporters are always trouble, they should be kept away from the president (in later imitation, prime ministers, premiers, whatever).

When there is no news, there must be the appearance of news so as to give the sense of activity. Photographers are invited in to take standard dishonest shots of politicians pretending to sign papers or shake hands. Cameramen are welcome because they don't ask questions. (Reporters are not welcome in "photo opportunities" for the simple reason that they are after information. Sam Donaldson, the obstreperous ABC correspondent, is *persona non grata* at the Reagan White House because he persists in shouting questions during what are supposed to be sterile "photo ops.")

The pencil press hates these contrived non-events, but the docile electronic jockeys go along because it provides their evening news programs with the phoney clips of politicians in the appearance of action. The politicians love it because it serves their purpose, pretending that a non-event is an event —except when it backfires, as it did Clark on his "world tour," as it did Marc Lalonde on his celebrated photo op before his budget in spring 1983. It would have taken a playwright like Pinter or Beckett to transmit adequately the surrealist qualities of the Ottawa outpost over the event.

While a snowstorm swirled about and swivel servants tramped along hidden in their April parkas, the smug Liberals, thinking they'd won a victory, only added further proof of their devious nature. Marc (Leaky) Lalonde added to his reputation for prodigious hard work and stubborn resolve a further dimension of heavy-handed fumbling.

Knowing that his predecessor Allan MacEachen had a deserved reputation for being too reclusive, too distant from the press, as finance minister, Leaky Lalonde decided to act the clown, getting his new shoes (another non-event) photographed and in cocky fashion flipping through his budget pages. He was astounded, later, to discover that the Hamilton TV crew that caught the few key French pages on the TV camera could actually read and translate the embarrassing leak.

Lalonde's reputation as the only strong man left in an asparagus-like cabinet was dented severely when he suffered a dubious loss of memory in the Gillespie affair. Now the man who brought Fortress Alberta to its knees turned out to be an inept clownster and—caught out—devious and smarmy as well.

While his prime minister, in defence of him, was putting on a slippery dancing-on-a-pinhead act in Question Period that would have any mother washing out a six-year-old's mouth with soap, Leaky Lalonde was adding a last-minute panic insertion of $200 million to the budget figures in an attempt to backdate his goof.

Explaining away his clowning, he said the action of the alert Hamilton TV cameraman "was clearly contrary to the spirit of the 'photo opportunity' session." Of course it was contrary. Some news seeped out of a non-news event! The smelling salts, please.

Because of this unprecedented occurrence, and the uproar in the Commons while the snow swirled about, the delivery of the budget speech itself that evening was in some doubt. Airplanes were already headed to Canadian embassies around the world with the official figures that The Leak and The Leader were desperately trying to change.

It cost the taxpayers only $200 million more to paper over Mr. Ziegler's flawed invention. The Liberals' generosity, with other people's money, matches perfectly their refusal to admit that the Natural Governing Party can possibly make a mistake. What's a million? What's $200 million to cover a finance minister's wounded pride?

Lalonde smirked in his "revised" budget delivery, as the Liberal lapdogs to his rear applauded in their stupidity the sinking of his reputation. Later, at a reception in Speaker Jeanne Sauvé's quarters, he was proud as punch, like a boy who had stolen his neighbour's apples and had gotten away with it.

Forget Pinter. Forget Beckett. Only Charlie Chaplin—especially because the scene of the crime was covered in snow —could capture it all perfectly.

Following the 1980 election, press coverage of the Clark "photo opportunity" tour was again blamed for the Tory defeat. The anthills were alive with the sound of outrage. If you picked up any letters-to-the-editor section in the country you found all these fomenting Tories, stewing in their own juices, having discovered the reason their Quixote of the oilfields fell on his own lance.

The reason, *mirable dictu*, had been unveiled. It was all because a clutch of nasty commentators, mainly armed with typewriters, did a number on poor young Joe, and a slavering nation, meekly falling in line, marched obediently to the polling booth and voted the way your favourite columnist dictated.

Oh what balm! What salvation! What a convenient escape route. For the sins and stupidities of the Tories, look not inward but at the scapegoat—the all-powerful press that decides elections and toys with the fate of the nation. Rationalization is a great art form. The Conservative Party navel-gazing, contemplating the illusion instead of the reality, is a rather pitiful spectacle to behold.

It is all doubly puzzling, this viewing of the facts of politics through the wrong end of the telescope, because there had probably never been a time when the press was less powerful in its ability to affect elections. Every major English-language newspaper in Canada, with the exception of the Toronto *Star*, backed Joe Clark and the Conservatives in the 1980 election. Practically every single commentator and columnist on the campaign trail—not to mention the meat-and-potatoes reporters—was openly contemptuous of the cynical, insulting Liberal campaign run by Pierre Trudeau and his packagers.

Little good that did anyone. The voters went their own blissful way, as always, and did what they were going to do in the first place. The abiding myth that the powerful press (and powerful press personalities) somehow hold sway over a simple-minded electorate is one of the astonishing fairy tales of our time. The belief that a Hearstian decision, arrived at over a press club bar, can affect in the teensiest way the polling booth is the thumb-sucking refuge, the Linus blanket, of the immature Tory party.

In 1974 the newspaper proprietors of the land, in their

infinite wisdom, stood shoulder to intellectual shoulder in support of the dignified (to the point of petrification) Robert Stanfield. We know what happened to him — destined to finish his political days wandering the sands of Arabia.

There are juicy examples cluttering the landscapes of history. Franklin Delano Roosevelt, the raging pinko of his time according to the rock-ribbed traditionalists, was vehemently denounced for four straight presidential elections by ninety-five percent of the American press — owned by good Republican owners. For four terms he laughed his way to the ballot box. W.A.C. Bennett, the shrewd old con man, for twenty years in power in British Columbia, courted the enmity of the four daily newspapers of Vancouver and Victoria. It was, he explained, like flying a kite. You can't fly a kite in dead air. You had to have the wind going against you. For a politician to succeed, he explained with a delicious chortle to a helpless columnist who raged against him, you had to have the foaming press against you.

The delusion, so believed by the frustrated and furious Tories, that the press can make or break a politician, is a hoary hangover from those days when press magnates were shamelessly partisan and a public could get its information and views from practically only one source. But one of the funny things about modern journalism is that the increasing concentration of ownership has not — unlike other industries — been accompanied by increasing power.

It may help the profits and the orderly balance sheet, but it doesn't influence the public decision-making process one iota. The voters read their newspapers and then do what they were going to do anyway. The days when a single journalist could swing or sway votes, a Westbrook Pegler, a Drew Pearson, a John Dafoe or Bruce Hutchison or Blair Fraser, went out with Rudy Vallee.

I blush to inform you, but journalism these days is one big service industry. Any readership survey will show you that the columnists with the boggling ratings are the ones who tell you how to change your snow tires or where to find canning lids. Ann Landers, with her meat-loaf-and-menopause

81

formula, tops the pundits every single day. To suggest that six Canadian columnists (who vote four different ways) can overthrow — or christen — a PM is highly flattering but, in truth, a vast insult to the body politic. The system, she just don't work that way.

Of more importance is what this currently popular myth reveals about the Tory party. It had very serious problems for seven years with the public perception of Joe Clark as a man capable of sitting in the prime minister's chair. The press didn't create those doubts. It only reflected them. The party, of course, didn't want to face up to the serious consequences of the fact that it may have made a big mistake in its compromise choice back in 1976 — and then finally conceded that it had in 1983.

One of the sad things about the Tories of the 1980s, a professional, full-time opposition party that could benefit Canada by being in power for a good stretch, is that it persists in this futile bleat that it and its then leader were defeated in the last election by a few nasty critics. Oh Lord, if only we had the power ascribed to us.

The real lesson of the Rover Boys Abroad, in January 1979, became apparent in December of that year. The callow and green Clarkians who couldn't keep track of their underwear on a world tour couldn't *count* on December 13 and lost a budget vote, a government, a subsequent election and, eventually, their political careers.

The point was not a fouled-up air connection or a bump into an honour guard and a near nick with a bayonet. The point was that a jaunt through five countries in twelve days, for a future prime minister, was a test of his composure and adaptability — and most of all, of the calibre of people around him.

Clark's failure as a leader of a party, as a head of a brief government, was that he could not attract bright and competent people around him. The Harvard School of Business Administration has a cruel, but true, maxim: first-class men hire first-class men to work for them; second-class men hire fifth-class men.

82

The general air of sloppiness and specific lack of travel sophistication that marked the Clark operation *three years* after he became leader was a foretaste of what was to come. Too stubborn and too proud to replace the incompetents and amateurs (or unable to find replacements?), Clark went down for the long count eleven months later with the same crew — the crew that had to be told by twenty-five-year-old aide Nancy Jamieson that, to their surprise, they were going to lose the budget vote that fateful December night.

Losing his underwear was not the issue that sunk Joe Clark. The issue was that he hired well-meaning innocents who couldn't organize their lunch, let alone a world tour, and revealed to a hitherto sympathetic electorate that it was indeed The Night the Kids Took Charge of the Dorm.

PART TWO

The Land of Odds

7 Wot is a Tory?

*"In civilized countries I believe there are no witches
left, nor wizards not sorceresses, nor magicians. But,
you see, the Land of Oz had never been civilized, for
we are cut off from all the rest of the world."*

What is a Conservative? It's hard for most Canadians to find
out, since so many Tories seem to have come from somewhere else. There's even a tendency for the Tories to go outside their party to find a leader.

The winner in 1942, John Bracken, was the Liberal-
Progressive premier of Manitoba. His only previous associa-
tion with the Conservatives was his father's attendance at
Sir John A. Macdonald's funeral in 1891.

Robert Manion, the tenth Tory leader, started his political
career as a Liberal. So did Hugh Guthrie, who was runner-up
to R.B. Bennett at the 1927 convention. Claude Wagner, who
was barely beaten by Joe Clark, had been Liberal attorney
general of Quebec. Another of the 1976 leadership candidates, Paul Hellyer, had been a cabinet minister under both
Pearson and Trudeau. John Crosbie was a member of Joey
Smallwood's cabinet before switching to the Tories.

Dalton Camp, of course, was a Liberal before defecting.
Bill Neville, Clark's chief-of-staff, was a convert from the other
party. If the Tories aren't coming from the Liberals, they
seemed to be going over there, as witness the spectacular and
suicidal defection of Jack Horner.

Tories are stubborn. Usually the leadership winner has

never run before (the exceptions being Manion, who won on his second attempt, and Dief, who was successful on the third of his four attempts). But that didn't deter such as Murdoch MacPherson, a Saskatchewan attorney-general who was runner-up in 1938 and again in 1942. Donald Fleming failed three times, in 1948, 1956 and 1967. Davie Fulton lost twice, in 1956 and 1967. Twice a Tory leader has tried to succeed himself, failing each time: Dief in 1967 and Clark, of course, in 1983, an example of a leader who choreographed his own suicide.

Tories are really stubborn. They seldom pick a leader who has had extensive experience in the federal cabinet. In 1967, two provincial premiers — Stanfield and Roblin — finished ahead of *seven* former cabinet ministers.

Canadian history shows that no provincial premier has ever gone on to become prime minister. Can Tories read? They persist in picking premiers: Bracken from Manitoba in 1942, Drew from Ontario in 1948, Stanfield from Nova Scotia in 1967. They all failed, of course. They are *really* stubborn.

The Tories are consistent in their failures. They stick to a pattern — they only appear to be prat-falling in random fashion. In fact, they alternate between eastern and western leaders.

In 1927, they picked R.B. Bennett from Calgary; in 1938, Bob Manion from Fort William, Ontario. In 1942, the convention went to John Bracken of Manitoba, followed in 1948 by George Drew of Ontario. By 1956 it was the turn of John Diefenbaker of Prince Albert, to be followed in 1967 by Robert "Big Thunder" Stanfield of Nova Scotia. Joe Clark of High River continued the pattern in 1976, as did Brian Mulroney of downtown Baie Comeau in 1983.

The consistency — as well as the failures — are actually boring. Each time, the second-place finisher is from the opposite end of the country. When a westerner wins, an easterner is runner-up — and vice versa (the only exception being 1942, when every candidate was from Western Canada). Roblin was second to Stanfield; Wagner was second to Clark; Clark was second to Mulroney — and so it went back down the line.

How can a party that is so meticulously *fair* in alternating each leadership between east and west, even alternating the runners-up, be such a resounding flop, a spectacular collection of no-hopers? It does, one must admit, take a special gift. These are special people, with special skills as underachievers. If Joe Bftlskz, the famous klutz who wandered through Al Capp's L'il Abner cartoon strip with a black cloud following overhead, ever came to Canada to join a political party, he would stumble unerringly to a Tory initiation gathering, held, no doubt, in a daycare centre that is empty in the evening, the heat/air conditioning on the fritz, the coffee cold, the sandwiches turning up at the edges like Joe Clark's smile.

"You can't tell an individual Tory from an individual Liberal," said Dr. Jimmy Johnston, the long-time Diefenbaker loyalist, "but you can tell a roomful of Tories from a roomful of Liberals. The Tories are all fighting with each other."

There is always some cabal, some intrigue, some dissidents looking for a reason to hate another portion of a party that resembles, like a fat woman from behind, several pigs fighting in a gunnysack. If it is not George Hees and pals trying to get Diefenbaker in The Night of the Long Knives, it is another portion of the party stabbing Joe Clark in the front in Winnipeg, which could best be described as The Night of the Cuisinart.

Dief denounces Camp who sits on a stage several feet away; Horner makes fun of Stanfield behind his back; thugs wreck the office of a dentist who is a Mulroney worker in Quebec; mysterious callers sabotage Manitoba meetings called by Michael Wilson; John Crosbie calls Joe Clark "ardently stupid" and the party rolls on, right over a cliff. There is no discipline, no cohesion, merely a collection of individuals who march (out-of-step) to drummers hidden in the hills, beckoning the faithful to form a firing squad in a circle.

The Tories, on their record have become the political equivalent of Sir Peregrine Henniker-Heaton, the British intelligence chief in the 1970s whose rotting body lay for three years in his study without the family noticing. You have to understand the basic free-form heating of English households to comprehend how such aging aromas can remain undetected, but the Conservatives unwittingly have allowed the same to happen.

Ivy-encrusted Tories who still have pictures of R.B. Bennett on their mantels tend to remain unchanged until they, like the One Hoss Shay, collapse in dust. A major injection of plasma is needed before the dignified blue blood of conservatism will once again flow across the sedate landscape.

Of Axworthy's quote about the party being "rich, thick and full of clots," at least the latter quality seems to be true. Only a collection of clots could win the greatest majority in Canadian political history in 1958 with Diefenbaker and then dissipate it so quickly. Only a collection of clots, given a rather lucky minority mandate in 1979 because of the distaste for Trudeau, would persist in a non-confidence vote on a budget without making sure they had the votes to win it, then call an election without the polling support to substantiate the decision.

The Tories, in their brief flings at power, act like a ham-handed new father given a baby to wipe and to diaper. They are nervous, unsure of themselves and don't know at which end to start. It all finishes up rather messy, and the Tories, like the new father, eventually have to be rescued by more experienced hands. They retire in mortification, not to be given the responsibility again for some time. (The father goes off and gets drunk; the Tories sack their leaders instead.)

Would the Tories rather fight than win (or make love)? Robert Stanfield suspected so. "Stanfield was against making speeches," says his long-time confrere Fin MacDonald, "because speeches were divisive. He said that if he made a speech in favour of heat, sure enough you'd find a pack of Tories out there somewhere who preferred cold."

Joe Clark, the most mild-mannered of men, was continually savaged by his own caucus even while he was rising aloft in the Gallup Poll, a lighter-than-air phenomenon, the world's thinnest Goodyear Blimp. Bob Coates, the veteran Nova Scotia MP who was president of the party, hardly spoke to Clark

— and vice versa. His executive assistant, Rick Logan, peppered Parliament Hill with regular leaks and slights aimed at downgrading Clark and, a very funny guy, was a National Press Club regular with his latest Clark jokes and imitations.

Lifetime Tories Peter Lougheed and Bill Davis, to show their high regard for their national leader, managed to find it necessary, while Clark desperately tried to save himself in the 1980 campaign, to spend their time in Hawaii and Florida, otherwise occupied. A provincial Liberal premier — if such an animal existed — who did not plunge into a federal campaign to help would find himself measured for concrete electoral boots. Keith Davey would leave a dead fish on his doorstep and he would get the message. (The Tories would eat the fish.)

Once in a while (like once in a while achieving power), the Tories do something unusual, something that goes against their grain. For the wooden-tongued WASPs of the land (and one should never discount their linguistic guilt) such an experience came in the 1972 summit hockey meeting of Canada versus the USSR. It was then that Foster Hewitt, the embodiment of all that was fine and true about Depression-age Canadian youth, revealed before the embarrassed nation that he could not pronounce "Yvan Cournoyer."

René Lévesque had hardly been invented, Robert Bourassa was not yet a public joke, but even the sports columnists were smiting their foreheads at the thought that the Moses of Maple Leaf Gardens was so befuddled by the other tongue that he mangled the moniker of the fastest skater in the fastest sport of all. It was a strange and useful scene: frozen into the memory of sports fans out there on the tube was the realization that a living legend in broadcasting had never bothered himself enough to wrap his tongue around the name of a foreigner who lived as far away as Montreal.

Inherent in that lesson was a bit of a guilt trip that trickled through the beer parlours. One end of the country, in the wake of Trudeau, actually began to accommodate itself to the pronunciation of such semi-household names as Chrétien, to learn that André Ouellet had some faint but distinct rela-

91

tion to omelette (though balking, in Anglo-Saxon stubbornness, at the glottal dexterity needed to master "Fabien Roy").

All this is a clearing of the throat to bring up the fact that with the election of Joe Maybe, the tongue was on the other foot.

Fair is fair, and one of the useful things about the election of the Tories (along with the destruction of the theory that Canada, along with Zambia and Tanzania, had lapsed into the realm of one-party democracies) was that the country was confronted with names that conjured up images.

It did Quebec good (not to mention Toronto's Primrose Club) to have to master the pronunciation of Ray Hnatyshyn of Saskatoon, Clark's energy minister, and the cool, competent Don Mazankowski who had never been heard of around the double-breasted martinis in Winston's in Toronto, but had been an observer at the United Nations, at conferences in the Caribbean and Poland and was Clark's new transport minister.

Steve Paproski, a jovial bear of a man with the girth of the *Queen Mary*, was one of only three Tory MPs to support Clark as leader in 1976. He is a burly ex-Edmonton Eskimo lineman who was a director of the Banff School of Advanced Management. One day when he was a bachelor, Steve Paproski was drinking with his buddy Gene Kiniski, who was the world professional wrestling champion (in selected arenas, on selected nights) and who has a face like four miles of bad road. Paproski, somewhat emboldened by the liquid, allowed that if ever he married and had a son he was going to call him Paddy. And Kiniski, pouring another beer, ventured that if he ever succumbed to the altar and had a son he would call him Kelly. And they weakened and they did, and so there are two young males now trodding the land called Paddy Paproski and Kelly Kiniski.

What we're trying to say here is that a country that has been long trying to master the other tongue and culture suddenly found itself, under a Clark government, faced with the reality of an ethnic underground that has always (shyly, but a bit embittered) felt itself ignored. The 1979 Commons dis-

92

played such names as Bill Yurko, the wandering spirit who was Lougheed's former housing minister, Paul Yewchuk, Stan Schellenberger, Stan Korchinski, an Alex Jupp from Toronto, an Elzinga, a Vankoughnet.

The elitist link between Rosedale and Westmount (which reveals more than anything that the similarity between Grit and Tory is keyed to private-school wives) was shattered by the ascension of Clark and his ethnic troops.

What was just as ironic was that the last-ditch Trudeau ploy for destroying the WASP-francophone swap of the governor general's post — appointing a Teutonic Canadian from Winnipeg — merely fitted in with the Clark scenario. Ed Schreyer, with his sparkling chatelaine who was once a farm girl named Schulz, formed his first cabinet in Manitoba with men called Cherniak, Uskiw, Rene Toupin, Rev. Philip Petursson, Burtniak and Borowski. When he arrived at Rideau Hall he brought a bilingual press secretary by the name of René Chartier (imported from Winnipeg) and a personal aide called Dave Chomiak. The next premier of Manitoba, an election or two down the road, is likely to be an MLA with the schizophrenic name of Wilson Parasiuk.

What was amusing was that the tight-mortgaged denizens of southern Ontario and upwardly mobile British Columbia —who provided Joe with his minority victory—supplied the votes for a section of the populace that previously had never been allowed access to power. Before, in the usual Ontario-Quebec trade-off for power and concessions, we had a belief that the ethnic minorities were merely there to be milked for votes. Ottawa, for the first time, had to adjust itself to a minority that had been patiently waiting its turn: Hunkie Power.

As one who has the commonwealth at heart, Dr. Foth sits down regularly, over sarsaparilla and a thin asparagus, with various layers of the mouldy lasagna that is known as the Regrettable Convertible Party. Such occasions are invariably filled with the snicker-snacker of cold steel, the blindsided gossip, the unguided innuendo and the heat-seeking grenade to the groin — all aimed at other Tories, some of them good friends, more often than not Sunday brunch companions, all brothers under the great umbrella of Sir John A., the Great Drunk in the Sky.

I stagger away from such meetings, reeling under the onslaught of deadly insults aimed at their brethren. It is their consolation, their religion, the cup they sip from, communion taken with hemlock, doctored with a touch of aspic. These are Conservatives at prayer.

A similar session with Grits is like a meeting with emissaries from Calabria come to deny the allegation that there is such a thing as the Mafia. Margarine would not melt in their mouths, and they swear their fidelity to Father Trudeau (who they see as an insufferable dilettante who was born rich and has yet to spend a penny of it, and who has overstayed his leave mainly because he enjoys power, somewhat like other people enjoy a shampoo).

They would never say these things in public, of course, let alone in the presence of someone they call the Merchant of Venom, and spend their time filling my pellucid ear with wicked tales of internecine warfare in the Tory camp — the same tales I have heard from the Tories.

The Few Democratic Party, of course, never dips to such depths of vitriol, it being pure of heart — and thin of votes — contenting itself with finely honed one-liners, the best of which being Ontario leader Bob Rae's private assessment that "Trudeau makes Judas Iscariot look like a team player."

The NDPers, because they do not have to worry about ever achieving power, can take the time to assess this strange band that sits to their right. The search for the definition of a Tory particularly intrigued one observer who sat for years to their left in the Commons, watching and listening to the collection of personalities who claimed all to be Conservatives. Mark Rose, a short and roguish former music teacher, was the NDP MP for Mission-Port Moody before resigning his seat in 1983 to enter B.C. provincial politics. He noted the various strains of the Tories extant: Red Tories, Blue Tories, Bay Street Tories, Right-wing Tories.

He found, nestling within the federal caucus, dozens of

other varieties. He claims to have unearthed the following — and suggests matching with the names:

*Concilia*TORY: one who tries to get along with all factions

*Migra*TORY: he moved to another party

*Manda*TORY: has to be a Conservative or else the riding wouldn't elect him

*Defama*TORY: the MP who most criticizes his party

*Reper*TORY: has the greatest collection of poems, jokes and anecdotes

*Dorma*TORY: he sleeps a lot in the House

*Conserva*TORY: the poorest tipper in parliamentary restaurant

*Perfunc*TORY: the one who shows up least for votes

*Ora*TORY: the biggest mouth in the whole outfit

*Preda*TORY: one who's always attacking the leader

*Inflamma*TORY: seeks to sensationalize triviality

*Explana*TORY: straddling the fence between caucus economic extremists

*Rec*TORY: progressive socially — regressive economically

*Direc*TORY: speaks straight from the shoulder

*Reposi*TORY: can really put away the groceries

*Regula*TORY: breakfasts on All Bran

*Reforma*TORY: a former member of another party

*Deroga*TORY: usually nasty with Pinard

*Purga*TORY: thinks it's only temporary

*Observa*TORY: now just sits there and watches them

*Audi*TORY: listens, seldom speaks

*Contradic*TORY: can't decide whether to run for leader

☐ JOHN GAMBLE
☐ ALEX PATTERSON
☐ PAT NOWLAN
☐ GORDON TOWERS
☐ JIM McGRATH
☐ PETER WORTHINGTON
☐ BOB COATES
☐ OTTO JELINEK
☐ BILL YURKO
☐ ERIK NIELSEN
☐ JACK HORNER
☐ MARCEL LAMBERT
☐ JOHN CROSBIE
☐ JOE CLARK
☐ STEVE PAPROSKI
☐ FLORA MacDONALD
☐ MIKE WILSON
☐ SINC STEVENS
☐ ALLAN McKINNON
☐ DOUG ROCHE
☐ PAT CARNEY
☐ DON BLENKARN
☐ BENNO FRIESEN
☐ JAKE EPP
☐ WALTER BAKER
☐ HARVIE ANDRE

Who knows what is a Tory? They would love to find out themselves. They even take surveys, which prove, as does the party's attitude toward women, that it is not really a modern political party. Indeed, a person who is not in favour of euthanasia, seal-pup harvesting, or being unkind to Girl Guides can only weep. One who supports blood drives, endangered species and mother's milk has nothing else to do but put his or her head down in repose. Those of us who favour a swift return of a Conservative government — as being the only chance of democracy being revivified in this constipated nation — can only watch and smite our brows in angst.

The Tories, the dear, blissful, nearsighted Tories, continue to do it to themselves. Look at their survey of their membership, which indicates, sad to tell, the exact reasons why they have been out of power some sixty of the past eighty years of this century. They boast proudly about this autopsy, which proves all we have suspected about the Recessive Concerned Party. If the Liberals had stumbled upon this same evidence, they would have broadcast it on billboards with their liberal slush funds. The Few Democratic Party would send it abroad in newsletters. Why the Tories would willingly print for public consumption the unalterable proof that they are so, um, *Tory* will forever remain a puzzlement.

The evidence in question is contained in questionnaires sent to the 650 delegates who attended the party's policy convention in Toronto in the spring of 1982. A good sixty per cent of delegates filled in the queries, which means it is an accurate portrait of the party regulars.

What they show is not just depressing. It is the proof, handwrit, of why the Conservatives are in danger of blowing the large lead they have in the public opinion polls. It is evidence of a party with hardening of the creative arteries. The typical Conservative convention delegate, it turns out, is a male between the ages of forty-six and fifty-five, who comes from Ontario and is against most of the advances of mankind since children were released from the mines.

What the survey proves, of course, is what you see every day sitting in the press gallery as you look down upon the blue-serge-and-grey-wasteland of the Tory back benches. The minds are as grey as the wardrobes.

It reveals that yer average Tory delegate sees no need for better job opportunities for women or minority groups. There are just three women among the 101 MPs in the party which, by all odds, should form the next government (if they don't publish any more surveys) — the smallest percentage of the three parties. There are no blacks in the Tory caucus, no Chinese, no representatives of the native people. Basically nothing but blue serge and doubleknit, with neckties, in the Gordon Taylor branch of the party, that are purchased in wall-paper stores.

Tory Incarnate, according to the survey, wants Ottawa to cut spending on daycare, unemployment insurance, family allowances and job creation programs. It fits. He wants the government, naturally, to reduce taxes on companies.

It is of no great surprise, of course, that it was discovered there had been a sudden influx of Amway distributors into southern Ontario ridings as Conservative constituencies selected delegates for the Winnipeg abattoir in January 1983. Amway, as we know, is the U.S.-based flogger of soap and cosmetics that features top American executives, our own corporate version of draft dodgers, who refuse to appear in Canada to face court charges that they bilked Ottawa, meaning the dumb Canadian taxpayer, of twenty-eight million dollars through duty dodges. There are one hundred thousand Amway distributors in Canada, a "reservoir," as Conservative MP Scott Fennell, chairman of the credentials committee for the Ides of January, so felicitously put it.

This country is run by a government that goes beyond the dictionary definition of arrogance, that is so contemptuous of the public, the press and thereby the whole political process that it deserves to be sent into oblivion for a good decade while it delouses itself, like a dog with a terminal case of fleas.

If you believe in our system, you have to believe in a healthy exchange of power between opposing parties — as in Britain, as in the Excited States of America. The reason so many people, young people in particular, are so cynical and uncaring about the political system in this country is that one party is almost always in power, in constant control of the leverages of patronage, rewards and punishments, the bastions for hacks and toadies.

Anyone with any sense of fair play wants the Tories to have their turn, their chance to appoint *their* hacks and toadies for a change, a move that would bring an entirely new supply of supplicants into the stale, mouldy Ottawa structure.

Instead? Instead we have an opposition party whose party regulars, meaning the party regulars at the party's policy convention in the Skyline Hotel on Toronto's fringe funch circuit, are proven to be retarded in their social conscience.

They are, by their own words in this survey, against increased spending on hospital care, medicare, post-secondary education and the poor. We would like to cheer for a Tory victory, but they really do make it difficult for us.

There are even personifications of their survey, like cut-out dolls, residing in their caucus. To the left of speaker Jeanne Sauvé, in the Tory back row, his shoulders brushing the curtains, there stands an angry man. His mouth is grim, his voice is urgent and raspish, like a cross-cut saw in need of oil. His suit is of that light hue favoured by businessmen in small Alberta towns, his tie shrieks for attention and affection, as if it needs stroking so it will lie down.

This is Gordon Taylor, the MP for Bow River, a man who is indignant most all of the time. He is forever on his feet, demanding answers, clarifications, explanations and apologies for the urgent and pressing matters that make him so impatient and upset. Gordon Taylor has spoken on 326 different subjects in the Commons between 1980 and 1982.

He has spoken on abortion, acid rain, disabled passengers on Air Canada, Bank of Canada Governor Gerald Bouey's salary, barley, beef, CN Express closures, the Calgary airport, capital punishment, children, Chinese-Canadians, farm labour, fishing vessels and Terry Fox.

He is an expert on government (dictatorial and power-hungry), grain elevators, gun control, kidnapping, livestock, metric conversion, NATO, the official languages policy and penitentiaries (Drumheller).

He wants to know about the Pest Control Products Bill, the Falkland Islands, postal rates, railway branch lines, RCMP contracts, the Safe Containers Convention Bill, the tobacco excise tax, young offenders, House of Commons' alcohol expenditures and the CBC.

Gordon Taylor is seventy-three. He was first elected to the Alberta legislature in 1940, as a Social Creditor, and was elected nine times thereafter.

> MR. TAYLOR: *We are prepared to stay here longer if necessary. But now for the first time in the history of Canada the government brings in closure. Maybe we should not be surprised because this government is becoming more dictatorial all the time. As a matter of fact, why should we be surprised because this government has a dictator as a leader?*

Gordon Taylor sputters with rage every day from his bastion of democracy in the back row. His metal-framed glasses reflecting the television lights, he shakes his briefing papers in frustration at the enemy opposite, pleading with Madam Speaker to do something about the slide of civilization.

> MR. TAYLOR: *What about the gun control he* (the Prime Minister) *brought in? Does he not want us to have any guns? There may be some reasons for that, but there is none to deny people the use of rifles and guns in this country.*

He was a school teacher but after the war purchased an established real estate and insurance business in Drumheller. Perhaps that is why Speaker Sauvé recognizes him so often, feeling that he represents a certain slice of Canadian life that has a hearing through his inflamed oratory. Like John Gamble, he never grins, never laughs. He has the disposition of an untipped waiter.

100

MR. TAYLOR: *I rise on a point of order, Mr. Speaker, because during the first half of the address by the hon. member for Simcoe South (Mr. Stewart) the hon. parliamentary secretary, the member for Ottawa Centre (Mr. Evans), stood outside the curtains holding his drink, I guess of coffee, and did his interrupting. If he is going to interrupt, the least he could do is follow the rules and be present in the chamber.*

MR. EVANS: *I am not afraid of you, Gordon, not at all.*

The last angry man was a cubmaster, beginning in 1933, for sixteen years.He was also a scoutmaster. In 1931 he organized and still runs Camp Gordon, a camp for boys not otherwise getting a holiday.

MR. TAYLOR: *Madam Speaker, the maps in question cost $5.95 from the Department of Energy, Mines and Resources. The photo of the Minister (Hon. Judy Erola) was included in the package. I admit that the Minister has a nice body, but it is too bad it is connected to her mouth.*

SOME HON. MEMBERS: *Oh, oh!*

Gordon Taylor is unmarried. He was the Whip of the Social Creditors in Alberta from 1943 to 1950 where, it is presumed, he developed his ferocious debating style. He has raised forty-five Points of Order in the Commons in the past two years. He has been a president of the Canadian Good Roads Association. He belongs to the United Church.

MR. TAYLOR: *Madam Speaker, I rise on a matter of urgent and pressing necessity under the provisions of Standing Order 43. Whereas the Quebec wing of the New Democratic Party, the Saskatchewan NDP, and the Alberta NDP have each adopted a resolution opposing any form of unilateral patriation, therefore, I move, seconded by the hon. member for Athabaska (Mr. Shields); That this House urges the Leader of*

101

*the New Democratic Party to get out of Mr. Trudeau's
bed . . .*
SOME HON. MEMBERS: *Order.*

The Member from Bow River, sputtering and tilting at
some obscure windmill, is now a bit of a *totem* of the tele-
vised Commons, his image on the TV screens of the land as
the Tory nonpareil, the exemplar of all that is out-of-date and
outraged in the party that is almost always out of power.

The image feeds on itself, a party of the 1980s still seen
by so many urban voters as containing too many leftover remnants of Diefencholia, filled with nostalgia for glorious times
past. The party won in 1979 only because of the electorate's
hatred of Trudeau but, sent back into opposition in 1980,
has basically the same caucus, unsullied by conversion to
modern times.

Marcel Lambert, first elected to the Commons in 1957
and re-elected nine times since in Edmonton, still hangs on.
George Hees, who seems like a tintype from an old edition of
the *Tatler*, plans to run once again in the next election because he enjoys the game of the Commons so much. So many
Tories enjoy the House because it is like a game of whist; the
Grits use it as poker instead.

The Tories are not real players in the game of life. They
go about their business just slightly off centre, outside the
circles in society that count. There is a fatal clue, attesting
to the pitiful fate of this party of outsiders. The Tories give
great parties: they are sentimental sorts, given to celebrating
most any occasion, lonely as they are for any chance to clink
glasses, smootch each other on the neck and generate tears
over eloquently delivered toasts.

This is most apparent to anyone who has had occasion to
sup at the Albany Club, a well-worn Toronto retreat where
old Tories go to die, or commiserate over another defeat —
whichever comes first. It is situated just about at the point
where King Street, in the shadow of the glass towers erected
by the fish-faced bankers who run this country, begins to
deteriorate, east of Yonge.

102

Finlay MacDonald's sixtieth birthday; a testimonial dinner for Dalton Camp; the tenth anniversary of the birth of the Big Blue Machine; a commemorative dinner to recall Robert Stanfield's charisma transplant — the weepy Tories love to don black tie and roll around on the floor in recognition of their past failures. As mentioned, all you need is the presence of Madam Masochism, complete with whip and black boots, and the lads would be happy. They *grovel* in failure.

The Albany Club, as one could imagine, reeks of dark mahogany, vintage prints and port as seasoned as Henry Kissinger's ethics. Dr. Foth's last visit there — by mutual consent — was not a success. The problem was the taxi window.

The occasion was yet another anniversary of some forgotten bitter-sweet Tory moment in history that the inhabitants like to drown in sorrow. Everyone in Torydom was expected to attend and, for some droll reason, Hugh Winsor, the *Globe and Mail* columnist who has now taken his dynamism to *The Journal*, and mineself were invited along, so as to lower the tone of the gathering.

Stanfield was to speak, Camp was to speak, Fin MacDonald was to emote, former Stanfield speechwriter Bill Grogan was to insult Stanfield, Hugh Segal was to insult everyone — it seemed a typical Tory evening. Knowing the monk-like nature of these things, I hit upon the bright idea of bringing along the lovely Beverley Rockett, a fashion editor who is the second-best dressed woman in Canada, just to demonstrate to the Tories what they were missing while sitting around moaning about R.B. Bennett's bad luck.

The taxi driver with whom I entered a financial transaction at the Park Plaza Hotel unfortunately seemed to have arrived in Canada that afternoon by parachute and was completely awash as to Toronto's geography, points of the compass, street signs and directions. He could not find the home of my escort and, while lost and communicating with his despatch office, refused to shut off the meter. When this oversight was pointed out, he grew surly and then abusive. Our relationship began to slip.

Having finally retrieved Ms. Rockett, whose blue eyes

widened in disbelief when she saw the mounting score on the meter (she thought I must have driven in from Hamilton), our chauffeur then could not find the Albany Club, one of the more historic pockmarks on the cement face of downtown Toronto. The meter ticked on and on while our beaten-up taxi meandered the deserted concrete canyons of Mammon.

By this stage, your agent, normally a man of the sweetest of dispositions, was beginning to grow a trifle irritated. It was a dark and stormy night and it was pelting rain. I suddenly spied the Albany Club, ordered our rebellious man to halt, flung a handful of bills in his face and, as we descended the cab, closed the door with more than my usual amount of vigour.

A most unfortunate thing happened. The window, no doubt somewhat weakened (glass fatigue?) by my muttered curses, shattered and fell quietly into the back seat.

Well, we made it to the gold buzzer of the Albany Club door, about fifty feet away. Arriving promptly, however, was the suddenly agitated chauffeur, who attempted to throttle Dr. Foth around the neck. This drew some attention. A crowd gathered. A street drunk, no doubt a law school dropout, advised my assailant on the details of a street arrest. My terrified escort was advised to flee inside, to an establishment she did not know, to hosts she had never met.

The taxi, by now rapidly filling with water, was abandoned, as it turned out, in the middle of an intersection, in the middle of the streetcar tracks (Toronto being about the last bastion, this side of Vienna, that still retains trolley cars). A string of blocked streetcars piled up, while this mild legal dispute went on, the puzzled and fascinated passengers peering out in the rain at the spectacle of my new friend grasping tightly the immaculate black tie of your correspondent, who was pressed up against the prestigious door of the Albany Club.

At this moment, there arrived the cream of the Tory party of Canada — Premier Bill Davis, Robert Stanfield, Dalton Camp, Finlay MacDonald — all striding along King Street, resplendent in their formal wear. They brushed past without a blink. ("I just thought," explained MacDonald later, "that it was another Fotheringham gag, staged for the occasion.")

My few friends within, delighted with the prospect of entertaining the charming Ms. Rockett uninterrupted, lost interest in my plight. Eventually, while the streetcars piled up, one of the few gentlemen among them, Mr. Art Lyon, a strong and silent Joe Clark aide who is a graduate lawyer, interceded, with the help of the Metropolitan Toronto Police, and a *modus vivendi* was negotiated. After I finally made it into the club, Dalton Camp said, "I've heard of Elizabeth Taylor's entrances, but this is too much."

This, it must be explained, is a metaphysical contrast. The Liberal Party brass, encountering — on entry into their favourite club — a Richard Gwyn, a David Halton, a Knowlton Nash being strangled by a strange, unkempt man would have sprung to his defence, knowing that their own futures might be in peril. Tories, being above such low self-interest, were concerned mainly about the effect of rain upon their tuxedos which had been purchased in 1938 and were in immediate danger of disintegration. Wardrobes, almost as much as their principles, are important in the party of indigents.

I digress. The Tories, when you view them up close — as they emerge from their many parties and policy conventions to decide whether they are going to have a convention to reassess a leader that will then require a leadership convention — are a scrambling pack of puppies, intermingled with aging and diseased mongrels of uncertain ancestry, ever on the alert for a new breeding formula, unaware at the moment that they must somehow import the female of the species.

They are lovable to behold (and incredibly fertile copy if one is a scribe), always eager to supply a new conspiracy, a new plot, some new intellectual terrorist, some new way to snatch defeat from the jaws of certain victory.

What is a Tory? In Canada it is a political child, face pressed against the encased glass of power, too wayward to find the key, desperate in the hope that the Candidate from Whimsy, Brian Mulroney, who has never run for nothin', can find the way inside.

8 A Party of Losers

"I am Oz, the Great and Terrible," said the little man, in a trembling voice, "but don't strike me — please don't — and I'll do anything you want me to."

The Tory party, having been out of office federally for so long, is a party of losers. Its mass appeal now and perhaps its greatest prospect for the future is that with the euphoria of the Sixties over many people feel they are, and feel safer with, losers.

PATRICK BROWN, ROBERT CHODOS, RAE MURPHY
Winners, Losers: The 1976 Tory Leadership Convention

Water finds its own level and a party that has been out of power for most of this century seems to attract people who take an almost perverse *delight* in losing. Perhaps Dr. Krafft-Ebing could have used his gifts on the Tories. They are the political version of sado-masochism, crafting their own whips, high black boots and chain devices that are usually seen only in the sailor-haunted bars of the Reeperbahn in Hamburg.

Joe Clark has had sand kicked in his face his whole life and persists in coming back to the beach for just one more hotdog. Even Dalton Camp, who eventually supported Clark in Winnipeg and somewhat less enthusiastically in Ottawa, labelled his own election coverage, in his book *Points of De-*

107

parture, as "The Wimp Watch" and referred to the advent of Clark as "The Age of the Klutz."

Erik Nielsen, who performed so admirably as interim opposition leader after the Winnipeg self-destruct, is a tough man who has never really recovered from the Campish-Torontoish tendon-cutting of his hero Dief. A lone man from the lonely Yukon, he was shattered by the tragic death of his wife and roamed Parliament Hill many a long grief-stricken night by himself, emerging from his solitude briefly to upstage new boy Mulroney's first day in the Commons' gallery by revealing he had married a Commons security guard (he had neglected until the last moment to let her know her wedding day). He's a hard man, hardened by too many years in hatred of the Natural Governing Party.

Sinc (The Slasher) Stevens is a financier who has never been accepted by the stern establishment of that arcane craft. He managed the remarkable feat, while establishing his short-lived and controversial Bank of Western Canada, of alienating both Western Canadians (who viewed him as a Bay Street slickster) and Bay Streeters, who were suspicious of him. Perhaps he learned his rules while supporting himself through law school by working as a cop-shop reporter for the Toronto *Star*. He, of course, is greatly credited with triggering the 1976 anointment of Clark by moving to him quickly after the first ballot (a then-prescient move that has looked less brilliant with the passage of time). In the 1983 race, he abandoned Clark and was with Mulroney from the beginning. A man who apparently can pick winners, he remains someone who can never quite make it inside.

Dief himself was the *Guinness Book of Records* markholder for losers, stubbornly running six times for office at three governmental levels and being defeated six times before his first victory. His whole career in Ottawa, *especially* after becoming prime minister, was spent in shadow-boxing turmoil with invisible enemies. He *liked* being a martyr.

Robert Stanfield — a dogged underachiever, a funereal figure in blue serge, persisted for three straight losing elections against a trampoline artist who took delight in swearing in

108

public in both official languages and who mastered the formidable feat of enchanting the public as first, a swinging bachelor, second, a devoted father and husband and third, a wronged single parent. There was no chance.

As a gang, the Tories are still well-speckled by serried double-knit ranks of Dief's old Cowboys, whose basic philosophy of life is that they hate the CPR. (It is an admirable conclusion, but lacks something as a rationale to go through life.)

John Crosbie, hailed by so many as a tragedy because as possessor of the best mind in the party he should have been elected leader, is, one forgets, a Liberal who drifted to the Tories only through his hatred of Joey Smallwood, who blocked his way to the top. Crosbie is a very bright man, but he fits into this pantheon of losers: a loser in one party, he has sought succour in another — and has finished down the track there.

There is the quintessential Tory — Marcel Lambert of Edmonchuk, known as "Piggy" Lambert to the kind scribblers in the press gallery. He was a Rhodes Scholar, nine thousand years ago; he was a Speaker of this here House of Commons (1962-63) and no one has ever paid any attention to him since.

Allan Lawrence is another refugee of a sort — coming into the Tory caucus with great expectations after frightening the bejabbers out of the Big Blue Machine at Queen's Park by losing by only forty-four votes to Buttermilk Billy Davis in the Ontario leadership battle to succeed John Robarts. Full of bluster and no humour — a commodity he shuns as if it were radioactive — he puzzled both allies and foes in Ottawa with his stentorian ineffectiveness. As solicitor-general in that brief non-shining moment of the Clark government, he has since distinguished himself by hoping, in the Commons, that Clifford Olson, the B.C. mass killer, be allowed loose in the prison yard so fellow prisoners could finish him off.

Dalton Camp himself was a Liberal, as he willingly confesses, going to the Tories only through disillusionment as a young man — and has been unable to gain a seat with his adopted party. The party that defies definition — the *Progres-*

sive Conservative Party — specializes in refugees, waifs, lonelies and those who have been bullied. You've got to think about that a lot.

Bill Neville, another original Liberal, was the chief-of-staff who provided Joe Clark with all those brilliant policy decisions that sustained the party in power exactly as long as it takes to produce a baby. "The Olympics can no more have a deficit," said Mayor Jean Drapeau, "than I can have a baby." Clark and Neville, innocents without a girth control device, should have talked to him. Neville was an assistant to Grit ministers Judy LaMarsh, Edgar Benson and Paul Hellyer before fleeing to the Conservatives. In 1974 he actually ran against John Turner in Ottawa-Carleton, vigorously attacking Turner in a personal manner throughout and losing by 10,940 votes (a "defeat that proved my loyalty, even if it did nothing for my intelligence"). His devotion to Clark as chief-of-staff was based on his hatred of the Liberals. That is not the most desirable (or useful) political motive.

John Bassett, the powerful media baron of Toronto who stuck with Clark to the futile end, has himself been defeated twice, once in Quebec, once in Ontario.

Hal Jackman, another Toronto millionaire who is almost as tall as Bassett, though perhaps richer (his arrogance does not have quite the same patina of humour), has a political record unblemished by success. He poured bundles of his insurance money off the back of a truck for three elections, attempting to beat Thumper Don Macdonald in Rosedale, failing each time. He early tried to back David Crombie for leader, undercutting Clark, but in 1983 ended up a strong supporter for Clark. You've got to wonder about that judgment.

Peter Blaikie, the hypersensitive past party president who still goes to Victor Mature's tailors for his suits, is a two-time loser at the polls to the undistinguished Liberal of Lachine, Rod Blaker, a former hot-line host and a controversial figure in the dark corridors of Parliament Hill.

Even the almost-famous Finlay MacDonald is a two-time loser at the polls, retreating to the backrooms as so many sophisticated Maritime Tories do, dazzling dinner parties instead with the eloquently phrased angst of sorrowful battles

110

at the polls up against the persuasive power of Liberal mickeys of rye whiskey.

Peter Pocklington got into Tory politics because of a losing
battle with his creditors (disguised as the Liberal government),
an instant millionaire who somehow maintained the image
of a put-upon orphan struggling against unseen enemies.

John Gamble, a tortured figure who was an invisible ci-
pher in the House of Commons, never smiling once in his
career, entered the leadership race solely for the psychic high
— like a hit of cocaine to the personality — of getting national
television exposure. He expired, in his leadership speech, in
the beautiful phrase of Peter Newman, "blowing through his
moustache, the madness of a hermit in his eyes."

Tim Ralfe, one of the heavy hitters of the media mafia
when with the CBC in the Ottawa press gallery, became famous (and made Pierre Trudeau famous) for badgering him
into the unforgettable War Measures Act boast that revealed
too much of a Trudeau we never suspected: "Just watch
me." The scales fell from the eyes of every intellectual in the
land at that one. Ralfe, joining the floundering and confused
Clarkians, became so bitter and undisciplined that even his
press foes worried about his emotional rages.

The late Claude Wagner was, of course, a Liberal, a Quebec crime-busting minister, then a judge, before being persuaded to become a Tory with the aid of a $300,000 trust
fund that was arranged by Fin MacDonald and Brian Mulroney
and administered by Eddie Goodman. This was the man who
almost won the leadership in 1976, blocked by the split-
Quebec vote with the same Mulroney.

Fast Eddie Goodman, the bagman who walks like a cher-
ub? Defeated the only time he ran, his famed powers as a
talisman and alchemist with the Big Blue Machine have never
translated into great success in the muggy Ottawa sphere.

Lovers of unconscious humour can always rely on Bill
Clarke, the terribly earnest and pro-hanging Conservative
MP from Vancouver Quadra, who is famous for his entry in
Hansard: "While I recognize that capital punishment has cer-
tain objectionable features . . . "

The supremely clever Hughie Segal, who failed in his passionate attempts to persuade Brampton Billy to run for a Tory leadership he never could have won, was engaged to Maureen McTeer before losing his thrust for the Ottawa-Centre seat. He retreated to be the brains behind Queen's Park and Mo met Joe.

These are all men, talented in their own way, in their own fields, who have one thing in common: they have been losers in their consuming goal to uproot the Liberals in Ottawa and to replace them with *themselves*.

Who are they now led by? The one man who has cleverly avoided ever placing himself in a position to be a loser. Brian Mulroney, if you look at his career, has been a remarkable success: a poor boy who worked his way through university, shot upward through Montreal's largest law firm, met all the right people, became a crime-busting royal commissioner, an acclaimed business executive, the first man in Canadian political history to capture a party without running for anything.

His ability to charm individuals on a one-to-one basis is unquestioned. Whether he can translate that to a group, an amorphous group of grumbling and querulous failures, is completely unknown.

Beautiful! The party of losers is now led by the one man who cautiously avoided the chance ever to have himself so labelled.

There are two types of losers one finds in the midden of the Conservative wreckage: those who dig their own graves and those who have them dug for them. We have two examples.

> *Some eras shape the men who guide them; some men shape the times through which they live. Our times cry out for a Leader who will respond to today's issues by giving them purpose and direction. We need goals in which we can believe and a Leader courageous enough to forge a pathway to them.* (Jack Horner campaign brochure)

We accept our small historical moments where we find them. One catches and freezes in a moment of time the watershed events of our life. So, as an anthropologist fascinated with political life, we are grateful for the amazing public event encompassed by the blood-red walls of the Tudor Room on the convention floor of Toronto's aloof Royal York Hotel, which has witnessed many a birth and death of ambition.

This time, January 14, just one month before the 1976 Conservative leadership convention, it is the burial of Jack Horner as a serious political figure in Canada and it is sad to watch.

At the back of the room is Horner's entourage. There is something flaccid about them. They are overweight, out of date, out of it. There is the strange phenomenon that one whole page of the slick brochure is devoted to the picture and biographical details of his campaign manager, Richard A.N. Bonnycastle, graduate of Ravenscourt School and now a director of the Toronto *Star*. A separate press release traces the modest lineage of Mr. Bonnycastle back to the Riel Rebellion. It may be the only candidacy in the Tory race where the campaign manager is competing with the candidate for ink.

As the cowboy from Crowfoot begins his act in Toronto, the reporters at the press conference stand with weary cynicism, nudging one another and sniggering at the accusation in the Horner press handout that Pierre Trudeau is guilty of "national socialism."

Toronto regards Horner as a rube, a redneck, a neanderthal and it's not often he even ventures into town. The exaggerated image is unfortunate because Horner, when you sit down with him, is not really a yahoo. He is an intelligent man—not the low-browed hayseed painted by the cartoonists—and he has a grasp of events that would astonish those who write him off as a loud-voiced dummy from the farm.

It's because he is capable of so much more that his performance this noon-hour is so ludicrous. Peering into the TV lights toward the sandwiches at the back of the room, he crudely hacks his way through his rivals. Paul Hellyer? "He isn't going anywhere." Flora MacDonald? Ah, the poor simple girl. The reporters name the rival, Horner has the appropriate insult.

113

Our next Leader must not only be a man whose vi-
sion we share, he must know how to make that vi-
sion a reality. In other times, a good Leader would
have sufficed; our times demand a Leader who is pre-
pared to don the mantle of greatness.

The name of Claude Wagner is thrust forward. Horner goes
off on a long detour about Watergate and how solid Republican citizens were the worst hurt by Nixon's lies and how we
can't let a Watergate happen here. Are you suggesting, I ask,
that there is an analogy between Watergate and Wagner?

Well, you see, Horner rambles about in best Crowfoot
obfuscation, the *Globe and Mail* had that story on Saturday
about Wagner "lying" about his famed $300,000 trust fund.
But, Jack, I persist, the *Globe and Mail* is not running for the
Tory leadership. You are. Are you hiding behind a newspaper
story? Are you saying Wagner lied?

"If he doesn't tell the truth about the easy things, how is
he going to tell the truth about the hard things?" The man
who thinks he can lead a party waffles and rambles, shambles and shuffles, flailing all around him.

Shakespeare has said: "Be not afraid of greatness.
Some men are born great; some achieve it; some have
greatness thrust upon them." Our times do not thrust
greatness on anyone; they demand it of the one who
would lead us.

Moving right along, Jack, you have this phrase in your
press release here. You talk about Mr. Trudeau's "game of
national socialism." Are you aware of the historical connota-
tions of that phrase? You know, of course, that the National
Socialist Party was the formal title of the Nazis?

"Is that right?" asks Jack Horner. "That's very good. I didn't
know that."

There is a stiffening among the sandwiches. The CTV man,
frantic, signals his cameraman to leap back to the camera.
The Toronto *Star* man, who happens to be Jewish, his knuck-

les tightening on his notebook, says, "Could we get this straight. Are you saying that you did not know that national socialism was the philosophy of Hitler?"

The man who would be king: "I didn't know it. I honestly did not know it." There is a long explanation as to how Jack Horner does not lie, Jack Horner always tells the truth. He didn't know about the Hitler connection, "but now that you mention it there are similarities."

By now, the sandwiches are tense with vibrations. *What did you say?* "Well, there are similarities." He's not saying things are exactly the same but, you see, there is his brother Hugh Horner and while he is like Jack Horner, there is of course only one Jack Horner and can only be one, he explains.

But there are similarities between the Horner brothers and now that you bring up Hitler and while I was talking about Trudeau, "yes, there are similarities."

By now the CTV man, sandwiches abandoned, is going berserk with hand signals to his cameraman. He resembles a beached yachtsman semaphoring rescuers. Jack, however, is unperturbed. Takes more than this to flummox a man from Crowfoot, Alberta. One does not know whether to cry or go into hysterics. *This* is going to be the champion of Western Canada in Ottawa February 22 when they count the ballots?

> *Jack Horner's vision, his experience, his accomplishments, his courage, the very man itself, are our guarantee that Jack Horner is ready to don the mantle that he must wear as the next Leader of the Party and of Canada.*

Horner, or course, lost, never emerging from the grave he dug for himself. Another Tory hopeful started out with a much better chance.

In 1967, editing a page of comment for the Vancouver *Sun*, I did a full takeout on E. Davie Fulton, then about to try once again for the Tory leadership, and asked a colleague to title it. (It is a classic rule of the newspaper business that one should never write the headline on one's own stuff.

Too close to the subject.) He decided on DAVIE FULTON: THE MAGNIFICENT FAILURE.

By March 1982, the former justice minister of Canada and former B.C. Supreme Court judge was spending his weekends in jail, in the Marpole Community Correctional Centre in Vancouver, sharing his time with bad-cheque artists and petty burglars. It is the most tragic story in Canadian politics.

E. Davie Fulton was always destined for the top. His grandfather, A.E.B. Davie, was British Columbia's eighth premier. His great-uncle was B.C.'s tenth premier and later chief justice. Another uncle was Speaker of the B.C. Legislature. His father was a B.C. attorney general and later an MP in the Borden government.

The tall redhead from Kamloops was B.C's 1937 Rhodes Scholar and then a major with the Seaforth Highlanders in the Italian campaign, when he received a letter in 1944 from a prominent Kamloops Tory. It asked him if he would allow his name to stand for nomination as Conservative candidate and concluded: "We hope you will consider this seriously because, as a matter of fact, we nominated you at the meeting last night." He was allowed home on leave to campaign, whirled around the cattle ranges of the riding in his kilt and squeezed into the traditionally Liberal seat by 177 votes.

When he entered the Commons, still full of the youthful arrogance of the Oxford Union and the fire of war, he created a sensation with his maiden speech. He became the first English-speaking Tory to deliver some of his speech in French and, ignoring the "truce" traditions of the occasion, attacked the prime minister so vigorously that he was interrupted eleven times by angry Liberal cabinet ministers. An impressed Mackenzie King leaned to his seatmate and whispered, "That young man will lead the Tories some day."

He foundered on the craggy rocks of John Diefenbaker's jealousy. Before 1956 they had been quite close, Fulton regarded somewhat of a Dief protegé. Twice he flew to Prince Albert to deliver Dief's French speeches. When Diefenbaker's first wife died, it was Fulton who was sent by the Conservative party brass to accompany the Prairie lawyer on the lonely

116

train ride from Saskatchewan back to Ottawa. It was Fulton who was the host at a dinner party in honour of Dief's second marriage two years later.

His sin was running against Dief in the 1956 leadership race, and the obsessively suspicious man from Prince Albert decided he had to cut down this clever forty-year-old man with the growing reputation. Once elected in 1957, Diefenbaker tried to neutralize Fulton by making him Speaker. When Fulton declined and asked for Justice instead, Dief waited for five days before finally agreeing.

He had attained more at an earlier age than any other Canadian federal politician since Mackenzie King. "He felt a real pleasure in politics," Peter Newman wrote, "and genuinely believed himself fated to influence beneficially the course of Canadian history. This was an unlimited man, strong in principles, outstanding in intelligence, and the best parliamentarian in the party."

Fulton honed his French under the noon-hour tutoring of an MP by the name of Jean Lesage. He had a bipartisan eye for talent, attracting to Ottawa such aides as Marc Lalonde, Michael Pitfield and Lowell Murray.

The more Fulton's reputation grew, the more determined was his prime minister to undermine him. Dief made Fulton the goat in the bitter loggers' strike in Newfoundland and handed his justice minister the humiliating demotion to the post-office-and-patronage wasteland of Public Works.

A demoralized Fulton decided to burnish his reputation back in B.C. while the obviously doomed Dief regime slipped beneath the waves. He accepted the 1963 offer of a group of well-heeled Tory businessmen, who set up the "Fraser Trust" to guarantee him an income for five years to revive the moribund B.C. Conservative Party.

The essential, for the Fraser Trust, was for Fulton, with his renowned debating skills, to get into the B.C. House in the first available by-election. An early opening in the little Rocky Mountain riding of Columbia, where an unknown Conservative had finished a strong second the previous election, provided the perfect opportunity for the onetime House

117

of Commons star to demonstrate his parliamentary skills up against the Social Credit woolhats of W.A.C. Bennett. The strategists of the Fraser Trust pressed Fulton to run.

He refused, his pride and family tradition insisting that he run in Kamloops against the well-entrenched and flamboyant Phlying Phil Gaglardi, the evangelical speed freak. He was trounced, of course, the Tory revival was over before it began and the Fraser Trust never forgave.

Davie Fulton, twenty-two years seeking the top, failed again in 1976 up against Robert Stanfield, incurring enormous debts in his lengthy leadership campaign. His law practice slipped. Putting up outside Christmas lights at his home, he fell off a ladder into manure-fertilized rose bushes, broke his leg, developed gangrene and almost died.

He was appointed to the B.C. Supreme Court in 1973. Then came the first impaired driving conviction. Then prostitute Wendy King, who brought down B.C. Chief Justice John Farris, published a book alleging that Fulton was another customer. An innocent Fulton, crushed by the publicity and a libel trial he had to endure before the case of mistaken identity was admitted, went back to the bottle — and a second driving charge.

He resigned from the Bench — before it was revealed that the man in Wendy King's apartment in fact had been Dave Rogers, an old Kamloops lawyer colleague who had not come forward to protect Fulton's name.

The broken man, an admitted alcoholic, served his fourteen day jail sentence in Room 4 of the Vancouver correctional centre, a spartan youth-hostel-style old mansion where he had to share the chores — washing dishes, helping the cook, serving other prisoners or cleaning floors.

B.C. has never provided a Canadian prime minister and E. Davie Fulton had a chance better than any. The political process broke his vast promise and, eventually, him. At the Mulroney convention in the Ottawa ice rink, he was present — seated in Joe Clark's box.

118

9 The Party of Grey and Blue

"Why should I do this for you?" asked Oz.
"Because you are strong and I am weak; because you are a Great Wizard and I am only a helpless little girl."

If you really wish to know the state of the House of Commons in relation to the real world, consider the fact that MP Pat Carney is the only mother west of the Lakehead. That is the best indication of all of the non-representative isolated male ghetto of the institution that rules us.

If you really wish to understand why the Regressive Convertible Party lives so long in opposition — and often seems so content to stay there — it's because only three of the 102 Tory MPs are female: Vancouver's Carney, Kingston's Flora MacDonald, Leeds' Jennifer Cossitt.

It means more than you think as an indicator of why Her Majesty's Almost Loyal Opposition is so out to lunch when it comes to the true problems of the country, so trapped in the past in its views of how society is constituted and what moves people. The Tories, in the anachronism of the boys' debating chamber of the Commons, are dinosaurs within the museum itself.

Canada, in its wobbling struggle from a rural hewers-of-wood country to an urban drawers-of-Perrier state, is uncommonly brutish in its attitude toward women. As late as 1968 — the year when the dream of Camelot had moved north and all heady idealism seemed possible — exactly one woman, Grace MacInnis, was elected to the House of Commons. The

119

descendant of the great pioneering CCF family (her father was J.S. Woodsworth) was all that Canadian voters could muster to prove that a new day was dawning.

Between 1921 and 1980, through nineteen elections, the Canadian electorate sent just sixty-eight women to Ottawa. Wars come and women can work in the factories but the political institutions, run by men, won't let them into the war of politics.

One only has to gaze down from the parliamentary press gallery at the assembled vests and collected closed minds in the Commons to appreciate how successful the masculine clique has been in preserving for itself the game for grown-ups known as debating-chamber government.

In the first fifty years since women were given the vote, some 6,845 people were elected in federal and provincial elections in this country. Only sixty-eight of them were women.

The number of women being persuaded to run is now going up — 137 in the 1974 election, 195 in 1979, 217 in 1980 — but it doesn't seem to matter much. The figures show that, over time, 2.4 per cent of the candidates have been women; less than one per cent of them have been elected.

The Liberals, demonstrating their true beliefs, once ran a woman against the unbeatable John Diefenbaker in his fortress of Prince Albert. Cannon fodder. The Conservatives, to show that they really appreciated their few female candidates, used one of them as a token candidate against the unbeatable Pierre Trudeau in Mount Royal.

> There was the Tory-inclined lumber executive in Vancouver who, he thought jokingly, told a service club audience — thinking it was just between us boys — that "if God had intended women to be equal he would have given them brains." When your ink-stained wretch relayed this homily through a newspaper column, the chap said to me, at the next meeting: "You *bastard*. My daughter is not speaking to me and my wife has cut me off."
>
> This relates, probably, to the celebrated dictum of the late Charlotte Whitton, the resolutely-unmarried

mayor of Ottawa: "To be considered half as good as a man a woman has to be twice as smart. Fortunately, it's not difficult."

The early, aggressive slogan of the liberation movement of the 1970s was that "a woman needs a man like a fish needs a bicycle." This has now progressed to the currently most popular rubric, Gloria Steinem's statement that "some of us are becoming the men we'd hoped to marry." I digress.

The CCF-NDP, with its democratic traditions, has always been the leader in accepting women into its structure. Dr. Pauline Jewett and Margaret Mitchell, both from the Vancouver area, and Lynn McDonald, from Toronto, sit in the small NDP caucus. The Liberals, concentrating as always on their fiefdom of Quebec, elected ten women in 1980, including Speaker Jeanne Sauvé. Three of them, Judy Erola, Celine Hervieux-Payette and Monique Begin, are cabinet ministers.

But it is on the Tory side, the party that didn't know what to do with power once it stumbled into it — rather like a cowplop — that the absence of women tells us rather more than we want to know.

Flora MacDonald and Pat Carney and Jennifer Cossitt sit there, as strange and conspicuous by their presence as they seem out of place in a party that isn't really able to figure out what to do with them.

In 1968, supposedly the year that we vaulted into modern politics, the pitiful Tories nominated only seven women in all of Canada. The Liberals and NDP managed thirty-six female nominations, with Mrs. MacInnis the only victor.

The other parties started to catch on; in the 1972 election they nominated seventy-two women. Five of them were elected. The Tories? Going backward, they nominated only six, Flora MacDonald the only one elected.

By 1974, the Grits and the NDP between them nominated 139 women, electing nine. The poor Tories, still struggling in another century, could find only eleven women to put forward at the polls. Flora again was the only winner.

For the 1979 election, the two parties on the leftward side

of the spectrum nominated 195 women and elected ten of them. The Tories managed to get all the way up to fourteen, electing Flora and Diane Stratas. (Jean Pigott got a seat in a by-election, but lost in the general election.)

In the 1980 election, with the proud feminist Joe Clark in charge of the party, the Tories still could attract no more than fourteen women. Flora and Pat Carney were elected. The Liberals and NDP, more aware of what was going on out in the world, nominated 217, elected fourteen.

The party has been a male domain because the males in it — those who are elected and those who run it at the riding level — are not the type who welcome women in their political world. The Tories in the Commons are largely of another era, another space. In the last century women have come a long way, now striding, in their knife-edge trousers, out of cigarette ads. These Tories still have a dribble of tobacco juice oozing from their collective mind.

Listen to Question Period. The Tory backbenches bristle with outrage at the Crow rate, boxcar loadings, picayune complaints and pettifoggery. It was a measure of Joe Clark's gathering peril that he was not able to change the character of this comfortable, plodding, out-of-date caucus. (Poor Joe, afflicted with politicus interruptus, did have Jean Pigott, the Godmother of the party, at work devising a recruiting plan for women, but that ended when her leader tripped and fell on his sword in 1979.)

Joe Clark, who is so young but seems so old, in two elections was not able to attract the younger, vigorous types who now dominate the NDP caucus and mutter, impatiently, below the salt at the arrogant Liberal table. With the exception of Toronto's David Crombie, the Tories do not have a single new face from the large cities of Canada who could be regarded as a modern man with modern concepts and a style that fits a changing world. A changing world involves those incomprehensible animals called females, who, if a party wishes to reflect society at large and thus gain power, must somehow be seduced into the system.

The Tories, flailing away at the supreme hubris of a prime

minister who indicates he simply doesn't give a damn about the sensibilities of those opposite him, claim that all their problems are due to the autocratic manner of the party that lords it over them.

That's not the essential problem. It is that the Tories, wallowing in self-pity, are not a modern party. One mother west of the Lakehead proves that.

A female friend once explained a source of quiet rage that would surprise most Canadian males — who go through their three score and ten in a cocoon of contentment. It was, she said, sitting before the idiot box each night at ten — as she and her husband watched *The National* with its clips from the House of Commons — and seeing a sea of grey and blue suits. Where was the other fifty per cent of the population?

Every night at ten, she explained with some bitterness, Knowlton Nash introduces to every woman in the land a reminder of why they are powerless politically. A blue and grey advertisement for female impotence.

The strange situation, which future historians will puzzle over, is spotlighted even more with the situation of Britain giving a massive majority to the imperious Maggie Thatcher, known as the only real man in her Conservative government. The daughter of a grocer, with her haughty manner and concrete hair, dominates British politics when the sceptered isle has never been more in need of inspired, tough leadership.

The serious thumb-suckers theorize that the British voters go for Attila the Hen because they have lost faith in their male leaders. If Britain's present monumental woes — antiquated industry, sullen work force, urban riots, a poisonous class system — were produced by men, would women at the top do any worse? It seems unlikely.

What is so inexplicable is that if the hidebound Brits can take the large leap and trust women, why can't Canadians? Could any woman, even with their alleged problems with arithmetic, make as colossal a muck-up of a budget as Allan MacEachen? It is impossible to believe.

Could any woman possibly be any worse than Pierre Trudeau, who took only fifteen years to steadily and efficiently wipe out the Liberal Party in the four western provinces, both federally and provincially? Obviously, no.

This is not the moment to go into, again, the phenomenon of Canadians liking not only male leaders but professional bachelors, like Mackenzie King and Trudeau, or childless men like Diefenbaker, R.B. Bennett, Laurier and Borden. (It has something to do with Presbyterianism, Jesuits and long winters.) More useful to contemplate is the fact that the Conservatives and the NDP are in almost permanent opposition status because they can muster only six females in their combined total of 135 MPs. Even worse, three of those MPs—Jewett and Mitchell of the NDP, Carney of the Tories — are from British Columbia, which for the past fifty years has had the strongest tradition of female politicians in any province. (It has something to do with warm winters.)

B.C. had a female Speaker, Nancy Hodges, thirty years ago, the first one in the Commonwealth, long before Ottawa got so excited about its daring appointing Jeanne Sauvé. B.C. has the highest percentage of females in its legislature of any in the land. What it means, overall, is that for all the women in this country who do not agree with the lofty Liberals, from the Rocky Mountains to the Atlantic, there are just three women in the Commons: Flora MacDonald, Jennifer Cossitt and Lynn McDonald, all from Ontario. It doesn't strike you that any progress has been made.

Israel, the most perilous nation on earth, trusted its fortune to a Golda Meir. India, the second most populous nation on earth, allows the wily Indira Gandhi to guide it. Britain, the mother of parliaments, puts Maggie in charge. (When the Polish Sejum [parliament] voted unanimously on July 22, 1983, the thirty-ninth anniversary of the communist government, to lift martial law after 585 days, the Associated Press wirephoto shows that nine of the twenty persons seated closest to Polish leader General Wojciech Jaruzelski were women.) But Canada, the most cautious nation on earth, still doesn't trust its women.

It's interesting that North America, the birthplace of the liberated woman, has the least faith in (or most fear of?)

women in politics. There is not a single woman in this country in danger of taking over the leadership of a party at the federal level or in one of the major provinces. Rosemary Brown gave it a rattle at the last NDP federal leadership convention, and Iona Campagnolo would add some spice at a Liberal one. Otherwise, silence.

The liberated ladies stalk the corporate halls these days with gold-embossed purse-cases. Their credit cards snap down smartly over the lunch check. They march off to Italy alone, they commandeer ski condos. They stride everywhere in self-confident pants, everywhere but into Canadian politics.

They almost dominate the Canadian electronic media, from Barbara Frum to Elizabeth Gray, Jan Tennant, Hanna Gartner, Barbara Amiel, Helen Hutchinson, Mary-Lou Finlay —and most every local station you can find. Margaret Atwood and Marian Engel and Margaret Laurence and Alice Munro and Mavis Gallant have made an international cult of Canadian fiction.

The real fiction of Canadian life — that women do not exist, do not form fifty-one per cent of the population—rests in Canadian politics. It's one of the main reasons for the cynicism and indifference toward Ottawa, with its outmoded ways, its Victorian traditions and tired stratagems of avoiding reality.

It's why Canadian public life is so grey and blue.

"The men run for office, the women run for coffee." It's been the standard complaint among the new breed of young businesswomen trying to force their way into the party of double-knits and dangling participles. Clark, for his efforts, wasn't able to change the look of his caucus in seven years, through two elections. The females even now are looking with some suspicion on Mulroney, who has the air of the locker-room about him, his personal entourage remarkably intact from the college days of twenty-five years ago.

"I don't preach equality, I practice it." That was the explanation Brian Mulroney gave when, after being elected leader, he made the surprise appointment of Janis Johnson as the new national director of the party.

125

A woman of high intelligence and great beauty, she is a stunning change from the usual pot-bellied party functionaries, smelling of old cigarettes and crisp slush funds, who ordinarily occupy that Tory post. By picking her, Mulroney was bowing toward a number of minority forces within the party.

She is from Western Canada — Winnipeg — where she has been prominent in Status of Women work and was chairman of Mulroney's Manitoba campaign committee. She is divorced (married formerly to the rollicking Frank Moores, when he was premier of Newfoundland). She is a single parent. She comes with strong ethnic credentials — the family roots are in the Icelandic stronghold of Gimli and the bloodline can be traced to Viking royalty. She is young, at thirty-seven a generational jump from the usual cut of fogeys found in her new chair. And she is a Red Tory — father Dr. George Johnson was a hugely popular family physician who was known as the conscience of Duff Roblin's Manitoba government, introduced medicare to that province and was thought of, by some, as the only "socialist" in that cabinet.

Although not widely recognized in the country as yet, she has known Joe Clark since both were Tiny Tories, working for Robert Stanfield in Ottawa. John Crosbie, remembering her talents from her Newfoundland days, wanted her to run his leadership campaign in Manitoba. She is probably Mila Mulroney's best friend and is one of the few close Mulroney advisers who can — undoubtedly because she's a woman — grow forceful with him in arguing when he's going wrong. Her admirers wanted her to run for MP against Lloyd Axworthy in Winnipeg and there are those who think she could be a future premier of Manitoba if she set her mind to it.

If the bait of Janis Johnson can't lure more modern young women into the Tory ranks, Mulroney will be eternally astonished — an affliction that does not often cross that Irish face.

Joe Clark had a reputation for liking strong women around him but, as the figures above indicate, he couldn't add to the meagre number of only fourteen females running for the Tories in 284 ridings. It undoubtedly had something to do with the confused and confusing nature of his leadership.

Clark has a quiet but strong mother, the now-widowed Grace Clark of High River, who has that calm and resolve common to women who've been through the bad times and the good times in Prairie small towns. (I recognize it, because I'm rather closely related to one of the same.)

Mrs. Clark, who once graciously and warmly welcomed me to her pleasant High River home where Joe grew up, has — understandably — changed her views on your faithful servant as my dispassionate critiques of her son and his ill-starred leadership grew more candid. Now, at Tory conventions, she fixes on me a ferocious gaze that would pierce a crocodile and, whenever I see her approaching, I flee in terror, usually into blind hotel corridors or exits that turn out to be the broom closet. When Charlie Lynch wants to frighten me, he announces Joe's mother is in the waiting room of our fifth-floor office in Ottawa, wanting to see me. I'm thinking of investing in a parachute so as to make a quick escape.

Maureen McTeer's strengths are well known. (Yet almost no one knows that the reason she kept her family name was to honour *her* cherished *father*, knowing he would be proud to have a lawyer carrying his name.) I am almost certain that, had Joe Clark somehow retained his leadership after the Winnipeg debacle and the Ottawa guillotine, Maureen was planning to run for a Commons seat herself. He is one of the few men who could have absorbed that — and welcomed it. They had a plan.

McTeer does not intend to pursue a career in law, after all her stubborn struggles to achieve her degree. I think she has raised her sights. There are tons of lawyers about. There are not too many women in politics who have viewed the centre at close hand, and with her determination.

There is more iron in that woman, says Dalton Camp, than in all the anvils of Canada. Maureen McTeer is a special person, greatly misunderstood, probably a minus to Joe Clark politically over the past seven years, a steely plus to him in the personal sense. Jo and Mo never looked better than on

127

the wilted evening of June 11 when they mounted the stage of the Ottawa arena together, took their lumps, looked the country in the eye and said farewell in gracious and dignified manner. While everyone else was kissing and hugging the dashing Mulroneys, Mila Mulroney approached Maureen McTeer in her ebullient European manner, primed for a hug or a kiss or some equivalent. Maureen intercepted the exchange with a stiff handshake, on national TV, that would have rocked the backbone of a stevedore. The outgoing MM meets the incoming MM. No bullshit. Straight goods. She does not compromise.

Maureen McTeer has been misunderstood because the icy manner has been contrived to cover a passionate interior. She cares almost *too much* to be in politics. The 1979 defeat seared deeply. I have seen her, over lunch, breaking into tears as she talks about the *unfairness* of the Liberal manipulators who sandbagged her husband. She cries too much. Women in politics who care that deeply do not last. Thus: the glacial manner to obscure what is beneath.

People forget that Maureen McTeer was only 23 (14 years her husband's junior; the same age span between Brian and Mila Mulroney; Mr. Trudeau was some 30 years older than his bride; is there a male need to dominate here?) when Joe Clark became leader in 1976. I remember turning to my buddy Marjorie Nichols, as the couple mounted the victory podium and remarking, "Looks as if she's borrowed a dress from Maryon Pearson." She was young and callow, though just as determined. Three girlfriends in Tory ranks eventually took her to Montreal, introduced her to the right shops and she has emerged in the past few years cool and assured in her appearance, a classy lady. When we meet, she usually says, "Still complimenting me and attacking my husband, Allan?" "Yes," I reply politely, stepping back smartly to avoid a knee in the groin. We get along, at a distance.

The measure of McTeer's influence is not so much about her as about her audience (the Canadian voter). Particularly in Western Canada, a reporter in Clark's later years still heard the tired bromide about any man who couldn't control his wife (i.e. force her to take his name) couldn't be fit for prime minister. She was in the forefront of the feminist movement. In 1976, it was news for a woman to keep her own name; today it is nothing.

Frustrated by her husband's Winnipeg Abattoir-to-Ottawa Funeral gamble, McTeer had an unusual and daring plan. She was to run for Parliament (and probably still will), a plan that would have shocked but made eminent sense. A liberated woman and mother, married to a liberated man, she aimed to sit as an MP while he sat as Conservative leader and supposedly next prime minister. It would have done a lot to open eyes and lead the way. This is a gutsy broad. We will hear more from her.

Flora MacDonald, the first woman ever appointed external affairs minister in Clark's hiccup-of-history 1979 government, says, "He is the first person I have known who is entirely comfortable with women in positions of equality."

Jean Pigott, the self-reliant Ottawa executive who ran her family's baking business, was the fourth strong female influence on Clark in his flitting flight through power. She steams into a room like a Mississippi river-boat, good-humoured and take-chargish.

She was the "Godmother" of the suicidal Clark regime, given the assignment of drawing up meticulous and fair patronage recommendations, her now-famous yellow books chock-a-block with legitimate and deserving Tory names — all ready for elevation — until the Clarkians self-destructed. It's one of the reasons he was junked: party regulars never forgave him for not getting the boodle on train quick enough.

Pigott herself, bitter at the accusations that *she* was to blame for the Clark indecision, deserted him in the leadership campaign and became a valuable member of the John Crosbie forces. At a crucial stage of the June 11 drama in the Ottawa Civic Centre, the Clark scouts were attempting to convince the Crosbie troops to come to them to stop Mulroney. A tired and tense Godmother exploded and ripped into the Clark emissaries, her frustrations at her one-time leader finally bursting forth in the steamy cauldron of Saturday evening in an ice rink (this is Ottawa).

Clark, though he couldn't attract more bright women as

candidates, managed to place eleven women among the top twenty-five jobs in the party structure. Among them was Nancy Jamieson, an antic, very bright blonde who resembles Lily Tomlin in her after-hours conversations (she could do a Joan Rivers night-club act with little rehearsal) and possesses a dead-pan analytical gift denied to Clark's cheerleader senior aides.

It was Jamieson, then only twenty-five, who startled the assembled brains of the Clark operation by quietly informing them at a 7:30 AM breakfast meeting on December 13, 1979 — since no one else seemed to know — that their shiny new government was going to be defeated that night. "Why?" Prime Minister Clark asked. "Because," explained young Miss Jamieson, "we don't have the numbers."

It was also Jamieson (by now policy coordinator for Premier Bill Davis) who, while the Clark forces bravely predicted a safe margin at the Winnipeg leadership review, won the $350 prize in the private pool conducted among CBC commentators by predicting accurately that his approval would hit only 66.9 per cent.

At her private farewell dinner in Ottawa, before leaving for Queen's Park, Senator Lowell Murray rose to deliver a few sexist remarks about the personal affairs of the attractive lady.

Jamieson stood to reply and announced, "Oh, we're going to play hardball? Well, let's play hardball." She then described her introductory interview with Murray, then a bachelor. She described how she had purposely come in her slinkiest, with a sheer blouse cut to *here*, and how Murray had drooled, hardly listening to her pitch.

"It wasn't until four days later," she explained, "that he learned I wasn't a twelve-year-old boy." The lady plays hardball.

Assuming that as a Clarkian she needs a year on Elba to cleanse herself in the eyes of the Mulroneyites, she has left Davis to take a Masters in Business Administration degree at Harvard. She will be a Tory candidate in a future election.

So will Barbara McDougall, a forty-five-year-old with

130

infectious dimples who has been carefully preparing herself for an entry into the arena. She worked as a business journalist in Vancouver and in television in Edmonton before returning to her native Toronto and a powerful role in the well-connected Rosedale riding association, where parties around Hal Jackman's pool are guaranteed to wow young party workers. A former vice-president of Dominion Securities Ames investment dealers, she now does consulting on government affairs and financial matters. She is the brains behind the David Crombie Rosedale machine and has run his last two federal campaigns.

A protégé that Carney and Pigott have been nurturing, in their search to find the right stuff for this male-encrusted party, is Ottawa lawyer F. Jennifer Lynch, a thirty-three-year-old of prodigious energy. Blonde and lively, she starts off each day by skipping rope for eight hundred beats, and once posed for a Participaction poster. She also runs an eight-body law firm out of a classy renovated house that is a bit of a local landmark and makes most every party in town. She's politically naive, but they're working on her. Any party that can encompass Gordon Taylor and George Hees could use a few Jennifer Lynches.

It will be interesting to see if the perky Sarah Bank, with her useful connections, will try for elected office in the new Mulroney era. A thirty-four-year-old food and personnel consultant from an established Toronto family, she made an audacious try for the party presidency in Winnipeg, supported by such influential party pros as McDougall, but was regarded rather nervously because her boyfriend happens to be Montegu Black, the older brother but second fiddle to the Teenage Tycoon himself, Conrad Black.

Regulars in a party that still includes men in that cautious combination of belt *and* suspenders understandably get antsy when confronted with the prospect of females who are not only young and pretty but rich too. It hardly seems, well, *Tory* to be successful.

The Tories, being twits, may not be bright enough to glom onto a secret for their future. They are the party of individualists. They have before them a new generation of women, spreading their elbows in the wave of feminism, who want to be recognized for themselves — not as an amorphous mass. The Liberals treat voters as putty, to be moulded. The "Pee-Cees", who are on a roll, have half the population before them, waiting to be wooed. Will they go for it? We shall see.

The first woman ever to have a serious chance at being prime minister of Canada has had a surprising personal experience with crime, scandal, murder — and betrayal.

Flora Macdonald is the redheaded girl from Cape Breton, a custodian of a position on the progressive side of a conservative party — a wing protected by Stanfield and Dalton Camp and earlier by Gordon Fairweather and a few other enlightened men who did not want to see the party fall back into the hands of the Colonel Blimps. She probably knows more about the inner workings of the party — having run the headquarters for nine years — than practically anyone else and has her contacts in all provinces — hence her knowledge of crime, scandal and murder.

The betrayal, of course, came firsthand in 1976 in the Ottawa Civic Centre when, as the first female to have a serious chance of become leader of a party that was destined to become government, her scrutineers counted 318 Tory delegates filing into the voting machines wearing Flora buttons. When the first ballot was announced, she had just 214 votes — thereby initiating the now-established "Flora syndrome," meaning delegates who fake one way and vote the other, an understandably sophisticated outgrowth of our over-polled, over-entrailed leadership mania.

The betrayal (which meant that Joe Clark, the only non-Quebec candidate finishing higher, at 277 — the highest Red Tory — would obviously be the winner rather than Flora) crushed her and she still hasn't recovered.

An angular girl of forty-eight at the time, she had done it all. The Speaker tossed MP Roch LaSalle out of the Commons one December day in 1974 for wearing a cravat, not a tie. No one dared challenge Flora when she first showed up in slacks. Now the female MPs wear what they want.

132

Unlike most of those insular Cape Bretoners, Flora got out and around. She toured Europe, lived in Britain and, when she returned to Canada, purposely set out to work for a while in each province before setting out for the next.

When she headed for Ottawa in 1956, seeking a job with External Affairs on the principle that it would probably lead to a lot of travelling, she got off the train, went in search of a YWCA and happened to go by the Conservative national headquarters. She wandered in, was put to work and stayed nine years.

Flora as secretary eventually ran the Tory office and developed an invaluable network of contacts across the country. When the increasingly eccentric Diefenbaker abruptly fired her in 1965, that solidified in the membership's mind that he had to go. It was Flora and her Maritime Mafia, Dalton Camp and the others, who engineered the dramatic leadership review that finally ousted him.

Camp and MacDonald were quite a team. Dalton, the acerbic, debonair Toronto ad man by way of New Brunswick, with his scheming and elegant speech-writing. Flora, the indefatigable organizer, with her fingers on key Tories in every province. They masterminded Duff Roblin's win in Manitoba, Stanfield's victories in Nova Scotia and a Tory win over the Liberals in Prince Edward Island.

Bell Canada almost sabotaged another Flora coup when Camp gathered his anti-Dief plotters in Kingston to lay the strategy for the overthrow of the Chief. Flora's job was to contact Tories across the land to determine how many delegates Camp could count on.

Bell Canada, however, grew quite alarmed when this unmarried woman who had taken an apartment in Kingston immediately ran up bills of $500 to $600 in long-distance calls across the country. It took some explaining to convince the telephone snooper that Flora was not involved in another type of business.

(Dief, the master of the heavy-handed *double entendre*, delighted in describing her, after he fell out with her, as "the finest woman ever to walk the streets of Kingston.")

After her time with Dief, she was one of the founders of the Committee for an Independent Canada and ran that office for a year or so. In 1972, she was the only woman elected among the 107 Tory MPs. She's straightforward and doesn't flinch. Her riding of Kingston-and-the-Islands contains five federal prisons. That's a lot of prison guards. But she remains resolute in her opposition to capital punishment.

Almost no one realizes it, but she knows Vancouver rather well and has a personal experience that is acquainted with too much violence.

When she made it to British Columbia on her know-your-Canada tour back in the 1950s, she became secretary for prominent criminal lawyer Tom Norris (later a noteworthy judge), in time to assist his defence of Vancouver Police Chief Walter Mulligan in a scandal involving senior members of his force. One senior officer committed suicide, another failed while trying it and Chief Mulligan fled to California — just in time.

Flora, who seems to have a gift for flawed characters (Dief, Mulligan, Clark), moved over to B.C. Forest Products — just as that company became embroiled in the scandal that saw Social Credit forests minister Robert Sommers sent to jail — the first cabinet minister in Commonwealth history put in prison for accepting bribes.

In Vancouver, Flora, as a good Cape Breton girl, was in a Scottish dancing group. She danced, as part of an ethnic dance night, at the Georgia Auditorium and her regular partner was a policeman.

The Scottish dancers worked hard and performed well and several days later Flora picked up the headlines to read that Constable Gordon Sinclair had answered a break-in call under the Granville Bridge, had stepped out of his car and was murdered in cold blood before he could draw his gun. His killer was Joe Gordon, step-brother to Dave Barrett, later premier of British Columbia.

"And he was such a lovely dancer," says the redhead.

134

10 The Party Men

"When I get used to my brains I shall know everything."

When you put it all under the microscope, examining the inner recesses of the political mind, you find that there is a disturbingly close link between the psyche of the Tories and the NDP. It is not, as political scientists instructing their university students like to think, a spectrum stretching from left to right. In truth, it is a circle, the reaches of red Toryism and socialism nudging toward one another. Not because of a Tory belief in the corporate wisdom of the state, but a belief in the stubborn dignity of the individual.

The Liberal Party of Canada, not marred by distressing ethics, serene in the knowledge that its only principle is power, is never delayed by such bothersome indecision.

It's interesting to consider why, for example, Brian Mulroney failed at the Tory leadership convention in 1976. His organization, his persona, the smashing and dashing young ladies from Montreal who adorned his entourage — all were too embarrassingly successful for the quite modest, quite financially careful little delegates who had saved all year for that trip to the Ottawa Civic Arena. They were, when you examined them, rather close in bankbook, if not exactly in philosophy, to the social-worker class of indigents who populate NDP conventions on American Express credit cards.

The Liberals, loving slickness and power of success above all, would have grasped Mulroney instantly to their tax-deductible bosoms — a John Turner with an even more sincere jaw. The Tories, suspicious of a conspicuous winner, as witness their whole record this century, shied off — revising their opinion only after seven years of thinking it over.

What distinguishes the Tory party, wandering forever on The Yellow Brick Road to oblivion, is the number of high-profile personalities who attach themselves, at key moments, to the struggling corpus. They stand out in the public eye, shout and argue on television, make the headlines with ridiculous or unproven charges. They are larger than the party itself and the party often doesn't know what to do with them.

John Bassett has the natural arrogance of a man born to money and grown to six-foot-three. He has startlingly blue Irish eyes and eyebrows that grow like wild gorse on the shore of Galway Bay and could easily nest a covey of smaller game birds. (The only man in Toronto who is a fair match for Bassett in eyebrows, height, money and arrogance is Hal Jackman, another enthusiastic Tory who is also almost always on the losing side. The only other true contender in the eyebrows sweepstakes is St. Clair Balfour, chairman of the Southam newspapers, but he is a Liberal.)

Bassett is the first man in the history of tennis doubles to win without moving a step to right or left, backwards or forwards, an affliction brought about by bad knees. He overcomes this small handicap by attaching to himself young road-runner partners. Usually former Ontario badminton champions, they are swift of foot and clock ten or fifteen miles on their odometers each match in relentless pursuit of the ball all over the court, while host Bassett, on his immaculately rolled clay court at his summer estate, Tyrone, an hour north of Toronto, stands like the Colossus of Rhodes at the net, swatting down anything within reach, like a bored man squishing mosquitoes.

After despatching younger opponents, Bassett, with vast amusement, wears his index finger to the nub phoning the match score to anyone who he feels would find the result the most amusing to the listeners — and degrading to the losers.

Now sixty-seven and gleefully boasting that he collects the old-age pension from Ottawa (that wouldn't pay for his sun-tan oil), he is married to a beautiful blonde, Isabel, who is a quarter-century his junior. Bassett created the scandal of the decade for the Toronto society gossip set when, sixteen years ago, as publisher of the Toronto *Telegram*, he left his wife to marry Isabel, who was then a reporter in his newsroom.

Carling Bassett (the only tennis prodigy in the world named after a brewery) is his granddaughter, and it is esti-mated by her agents that, at fifteen, she will earn $1.5 mil-lion from tennis and endorsements in the next year. When she made it to the Wimbledon quarter-finals, Bassett's CFTO TV station announced it would carry the match live at the unusual time of a weekday morning. When I said to Bassett that it looked like a personal order from him, he beamed and said, "Of course. What's the use of power unless you use it?"

Carling's father is Johnny F. Bassett, the sports entrepre-neur whose first sign of talent came when, for a Toronto teen television show, he discovered the beauty of Carole Taylor, now Mrs. Art Phillips of Vancouver. He is married to Susan Carling, who is from one end of the beer-makers Carling O'Keefe which, when you think about it, is another merger.

John Bassett was a major in the Seaforth Highlanders in the latest of the great wars and offered himself to the Conser-vatives immediately on returning in 1945. He ran in the Que-bec seat of Sherbrooke in the Eastern Townships, home of the family newspaper and the weekend retreat for the horsey Anglo set down from Montreal. He was defeated.

By now a famous and powerful newspaper tycoon, he tried again in Toronto Spadina riding in 1962. He was defeated. He feels that if he had been elected he would eventually have been prime minister, since Dief was on the slide to the end. Bassett, who was quite close to Dief at one stage, says he has seldom seen "such an imaginative liar."

When Joe Clark was elected, he sought out the advice of

the outspoken Bassett, who knew all the brokers in the party, before making up his cabinet. Bassett told him to make sure of the fealty of the established core of the party by, in a natural move, making George Hees—who had won battle honours as an infantry brigade major in the war—the Veteran Affairs Minister. Also, urged Bassett, give the durable Alvin Hamilton "one of those western jobs I don't know much about"—responsibility for the wheat board.

Instead, to Bassett's astonishment, Clark gave Victoria's Allan McKinnon (one of only three MPs to support him in his leadership race) not only Defence but doubled him up with Veteran Affairs. Bassett gesticulates in amazement. "He should have been *inventing* new portfolios so as to spread the rewards around. Not doubling up!

"Christ! He made Allan Lawrence solicitor-general. If he'd been smart he would have made one guy *solicitor*! And another guy *general*!"

Bassett supported Clark at the Mulroney convention for, he says, two reasons. He felt sorry for him because of the unremitting press and opposition ridicule and he felt his conduct was such that he deserved a second chance. He chuckles as he recalls that Clark didn't put into action a single suggestion he had made at their 1979 meeting.

Like Bassett, Hal Jackman is a large millionaire with an unfulfilled desire, for some strange reason, to become a lowly Member of Parliament. Why someone would voluntarily wish to give up a large home in leafy Rosedale in Toronto, where the rich interbreed, give up the clubs and countinghouses and the insurance industry to sit long hours in the House of Commons, listening to Gordon Taylor orate, and suffer through the insularity of Ottawa life, is a mystery.

However, Jackman three times in a row tried to unseat Donald (Thumper) Macdonald in the Rosedale ghetto, failing each time. Thumper, grown tired of the slogging life of a cabinet minister and bored with waiting for Pierre Eternally Himself to grow up, eventually gave up the seat Jackman coveted and is himself back in Toronto, setting a record mark for the slowest-starting royal commission in history, the ponderous probe of the economy that will pay him $850 a day to figure out what was done wrong five years ago and that promises to report, at the earliest, by the end of the century.

Jackman, who is the Tory bagman in Toronto, agrees in advance with Grit bagman Senator John Godfrey how much they are going to hit the corporate giants for, since this is the way our democracy is financed. They sometimes drive off together to meet their "clients," bags in hand, one bleu, one rouge.

As chairman of the Empire Life Insurance Co., Jackman in 1978 was backing tiny imperfect David Crombie for prime minister but then, keeping his political record unblemished with success, was a vociferous backer of Clark at both Winnipeg and Ottawa.

It is not for a mere scribbler to know why, but there is something about politics that brings out, in powerful men like Jackman or Bassett or Conrad Black or Peter Pocklington, the same instincts that move rich men to treat sport franchises like tinker toys and to become boys again. One has only to gaze, with wonderment, at the spectacle of the elongated Jackman, in the midst of the frenzied cheering at the Winnipeg Convention Centre in January 1983, merrily whacking the banners of ABC (Anybody But Clark) teenagers with his own huge poster, trying to blot out their attempts to make it in front of the TV cameras. The impression, for all the world, was of a boy in his private school dorm, whaling away in a pillow fight — except that it was all being done by this fifty-fivish millionaire in the compulsory pinstripe uniform.

Any discussion of the outstanding eccentrics of the Tory story must include Richard Hatfield, the quite remarkable premier of New Brunswick, the only bachelor among our provincial leaders. Stories about him fuel the late-night sessions. The most popular one currently delighting the cocktail circuit is the one about the night Dick Hatfield baked his cat.

The story, which has been circulating and gathering credence for some years now, has Hatfield coming home late

139

one rainy night to his beautifully decorated home in Fredericton to find his loving cat wet and bedraggled on the doorstep. Thinking to warm it, he turned on the oven and lowered the door to let out a shaft of heat. Being forgetful, he went to sleep, but was awakened in the middle of the night by an acrid smell. The cat, seeking warmth, had leaped upon the oven door, which snapped shut. Fricasséed pussy, as we say.

Hatfield, defensive about the wide circulation of the story, says it is not true — although he does concede there is faint source for the true story. The celebrated tale, he explains, comes from when he was a boy. He didn't bake his cat. He did, though, put his pet rabbit in the deep freeze. I think I prefer the first story.

The first remarkable thing about Alan Eagleson, the Finger, as he is known to millions of Canadians who witnessed on television his digital salute to the crowd in Moscow in that memorable hockey series against The Bad Guys — is that to this day he denies ever doing it. This is hubris supreme. All Canada saw it, but Alan Eagleson denies it. This is Eagleson.

The second thing to remember about him is that at least until recently his ambition was to become prime minister of Canada. Humility is not his second name. In fact, he doesn't know how to spell it. If he ever made it, they would have to change the rules for table manners at 24 Sussex Drive. Eagleson at dinner is an unguided muscle, as noisy as a motorbike-in-heat and as uncontrollable as a three-year-old. Hostesses in Toronto have had to have their entire drawing room ceilings repainted after his visits. His colourful use of some of the more basic forms of English would be more appropriate for longshoremen.

Oscar Wilde said of Frank Harris, his outrageously behaved contemporary, that Harris "had been in all the great homes of England. Once." Eagleson, in his playful manner, is trying for the same record in Toronto circles.

Several years ago, in a Broadway theatre, I was attempting to enjoy *Sugar Babies*, the raunchy vaudeville musical that starred Mickey Rooney and the gorgeous sixty-year-old gams of Ann Miller. By halfway through the first act the enjoyment of the corny jokes and the overdone ribaldry was hampered by the raucous laughter, at high decibels, emanating from the row behind. The author of the uncontrollable, nonstop laughter, who soon was gathering more attention than the action onstage, obviously was some rube vacuum cleaner salesman in from Omaha for a weekend in the Big Apple.

But there seemed something faintly familiar in the sound of the guffaws, which were longer even than Ann Miller's legs. I turned around. It was Eagleson with wife Nancy (the only person who can cope with his kinetic energy and four-letter approach to life).

He has a lust for life, like Bassett, like Goodman, like Fin MacDonald — unlike so many dessicated Liberals in their six-piece suits, their eyes on an appointment to the Freshwater Fish Marketing Corporation. (It does exist. Based in Winnipeg, it contains eleven appointees, and refuses to divulge to a reporter how much they are paid. *Wonderful!*)

In the 1976 leadership race, Mulroney-supporter Eagleson, as Ontario party president, managed to deny a delegate seat to rising newspaper chain proprietor Douglas Bassett, son of John, because he was suspected of leaning toward Claude Wagner. Douglas Bassett was understandably enraged. He was one-third of an informal power bloc, the other members being Fred Eaton, the brightest of the department store heirs, and Conrad Black. The Eagleson ploy helped nudge them — and their chequebooks — into the Wagner camp. When Wagner came off the stage in the Ottawa Civic Arena after his 1976 candidacy speech, he hugged Conrad Black.

By 1983, Eagleson had abandoned Mulroney for Clark, explaining that the boy from Baie Comeau had had his chance to run in both the 1979 and 1980 elections and, by backing away, had disqualified himself in the eyes of the combative Eagleson (who was once Bobby Orr's mentor and protector-lawyer but now they have fallen out — they do not speak).

Eagleson intruded himself in the 1983 race by stating that Mulroney had been "afraid" to run, his alleged source being a conversation over a drink in a Montreal bar with Michel Cogger, Mulroney's closest aide. This caused the usual flurry

141

of denials and countercharges in the public prints, always useful when the Tories are trying to hang in there together in front of the wondering public.

The problem with the Regressive Convertibles is epitomized by Eagleson, a flamboyant character who keeps his chin tucked in carefully when dealing with the Big Blue Machine, but erupts into a headline-slinger whenever a federal leadership contest hovers on the horizon. The federal party, being weak, cannot discipline or keep under wraps powerful provincial brokers who are driven by ego and/or mischief. It is giddy with self-attention, the cake flying and the candles persisting in going out.

Eddie Goodman is an antic elf, a Tory who got smart in 1945 and has benefited ever since. Returning filled with idealism (he landed in Europe on D-Day, was wounded twice, three times was blown out of his tanks), he ran for the Ontario Tories and was defeated. He never made the same mistake again.

If you're a Tory, you're almost always out of power federally; better to become a backroom baron provincially instead. Fast Eddie is a pint-sized version of Jack Webster, vibrations jangling all the time. He cannot remain still, either his tongue or his mind. His motor is running constantly.

His immigrant grandfather sold pots and pans from a horse-drawn cart. Today, high in the glass canyons of Toronto, Goodman has fifty lawyers, in the firm he and his father founded. His home in Forest Hill boasts a superb collection of contemporary Canadian art; his estate in the Caledon Hills holds his riding horses; his ski chalet at Collingwood overlooks the modest slopes that produced Steve Podborski, and the joint he shares in Palm Beach with his friend, Ontario Supreme Court Judge Charles Dubin, supplies his tan. Hustle and power-broking have their rewards.

Fast Eddie is an example of the problem that plagues the federal Tories: most of their muscle is contained in provincial satraps, princes from the political boondocks.

Goodman is an unquestioned power in the murkey backwaters of Ontario's Big Blue Machine, the operation that sustains the longest reign of a democratically elected government — forty years — a record surpassed not even by the equally vigilant administrators of Albania. When a Queen's Park backbencher by the name of John Robarts was about to resign because he saw no sign of advancement, it was Fast Eddie who worked his magic to persuade the austere Premier Leslie Frost to downgrade his feelings about Robarts' drinking and to put him in cabinet. It was at Goodman's house that Robarts made the decision to run for premier in 1961.

In 1975, Goodman was shattered when his twenty-year-old daughter Joanne was killed in a car accident. It was a tragedy for Goodman; for Ontario it meant a seat-belt law. He went to Bill Davis, convinced him of the necessity, and Davis pushed the law through.

It was Fast Eddie who put together the money that launched the Toronto *Sun* when John Bassett closed the Toronto *Telegram* and sold the subscription list to the Toronto *Star* for $10 million. He thus accomplished the unusual feat of making millionaires, through their founding shares, of two working journalists, *Tely* stalwarts Peter Worthington and Doug Creighton. Former editor Worthington, who carries on his own the burden of turning back worldwide communism, wears his wealth like a packsack of lumpy rocks, not knowing what to do with it, slightly ashamed of it. He gazes askance at friends like Bassett, staring at them at length, wondering how to acquire the gift to *enjoy* his money. He will never learn the secret (just as Bassett could never unlearn it). Creighton, on the other hand, is slightly amused by the whole happenstance and skates through life with a fey smile, like a man who has inherited a dirigible full of martinis and is not going to question the source.

Goodman, the leprechaun with the lively grey matter, is an interesting mixture, an angel for the National Ballet, a founding member of the Committee for an Independent Canada (this being the only country in the world having to start a movement to save itself from Coca-Colanization) but a man who broke with Dief on the issue of nuclear weapons in Canada, Goodman being in favour of them. However, he came back to be Diefenbaker's campaign chairman for the 1965 election, wheeling and dealing in his familiar slush fund neighbourhood.

Jimmy Johnston, the Tory national director, remembered: "During the campaign, from time to time, I would be hurrying about Toronto when a telephone call from Goodman would catch me. 'You've got $40,000 more. Spend it this afternoon,' he would say."

Goodman, for all his involvement in the chauvinist playpen of Queen's Park, has played a key, if not *the* key, role in both of the last two Conservative leadership battles. It was Fast Eddie as the bagman, as arranger of the important Tory slush funds, who made the arrangements, and carried through the payments, of $300,000 to Claude Wagner, the Liberal-turned judge, to come off the Bench and enter the Conservative Party in Quebec with Stanfield's approval — and eventually lose, only narrowly, the party leadership to Joe Clark in 1976.

Goodman has always refused all comment on his role in that caper, citing lawyer-client confidentiality. The point is that without Wagner to split the Quebec vote, Brian Mulroney might well have been chosen leader in that convention. (Even younger, even less experienced, even more vulnerable to the MacEachen-Coutts-Trudeau wiles, Mulroney could have had his career ruined as quickly as was Clark's.)

In 1983, it was Fast Eddie who was the strongest force convincing Bill Davis not to run for the leadership — against the gung-ho urgings of such as Hughie Segal, the shrewd strategist, and ad-man Norm Atkins, Dalton Camp's brother-in-law partner. It was sixty-four-year-old Goodman who persuaded Davis (possessor of the happy home life that Robarts did not enjoy) that he didn't need the aggravation and hassle of Ottawa and its voracious rat pack of journalists. Mulroney might not be a leader today, and supposedly the next prime minister, if Fast Eddie had not laid his lisping charm on the inscrutable Davis.

Therein lies the problem of the castrated federal Tories, importing their testicles every time they have an incestuous

144

leadership feud, bringing in the big butter-and-egg men from the provinces to do the dirty work. They overshadow the feckless wonders of Ottawa.

The Liberals, by contrast, keep a rein on *their* personality *wunderkind*. When John Turner, after leaving Trudeau's cabinet in a huff (a huff with white sidewalls and a raccoon-tail on the aerial), delivered an "off-the-record" speech critical of his comrades at the Primrose Club and later distributed a newsletter nagging at new finance minister Jean Chrétien, the reaction was swift. John Turner, one has noticed, has not been heard from, in print or voice — critical of his party — since.

The Grits have a way of silencing their own. The Tories can't.

The Tories do, however, have personalities they try to *hide*, a contradiction in terms, somewhat like a charismatic Clark, or a humble Mulroney, a tall David Crombie, a contrite Peter Blaikie, a non-grinning Bill Davis. In 1976 the Mulroney camp was terrified that the press would get wind of the fact that Peter White, a long-time Wagner supporter, had switched camps and was working for the boy from Baie Comeau. White's sin was that he was a partner, in ownership of the Sterling chain of small newspapers, with Conrad Black, whose eminently tycoonish image was deemed to be counterproductive. White spent the leadership convention in Ottawa's Embassy Hotel, the Mulroney headquarters, and he was registered in his wife's name. Mary White supported Clark.

In 1983, White was still regarded as dicey material, as if he had been found radioactive by a geiger counter, and emerged in Mulroney's suite at the Chateau Laurier only on the Saturday night of the victory.

The Mulroneyites are nervous about the press linking their tiger with corporate connections, and such dangerous names as Black and Desmarais are treated with the jumpiness encountered with a mention of AIDS.

One who is not hidden at all is the ineffable Finlay MacDonald, out of Halifax but now residing in the finest restaurants and watering holes in the land, a man who looks like a former fashion editor of *Esquire* while possessing the tongue of Gore Vidal. His hair, formerly grey flannel, is now as white as that of Santa Claus — though the sixty-year-old Finlay is thinner. He escorts women young enough to babysit his suits and is never mussed, giving the impression at all times, even on the tennis court, that Fred Astaire is his tailor.

MacDonald is unusual in that, considering the usual pig-stabbing nature of the party, he has been able to manage the dangerous portage through three leaders. He was a confidant, and worshipper, of Stanfield. He came into the office of Clark and his Boy Amateurs — too late in the game to save Clark — as a senior advisor on the way to the Winnipeg Abattoir. And Mulroney, discarding for once his locker-room obsession for good ole boys from campus days, has wisely hired the guile and case-hardened political smarts of Fin.

MacDonald, whatever devious ploys he recommends in private to the slow-footed leaders he was early encumbered with, is most famous as a raconteur. A broadcaster by trade, he is one of those unusual men, in our illiterate time, who speaks in sentences and paragraphs. (He shares this gift with Dalton Camp.) You can actually hear the punctuation. When Fin sets out on a carefully crafted tale of political intrigue and treachery, resurrected from some dim Maritimes past, a listener has only to close his or her eyes and the ear can detect the apostrophes, commas, semi-colons, exclamation marks and parentheses that decorate the monologue — not to mention the hyperbole and irony that decorate the syntax.

When one is trapped in a room with such Maritimes Mafia as MacDonald, Camp, Flora MacDonald (larded with a momentary defector like Senator Alasdair Graham, a Grit with a sense of humour), one realizes why that end of the country remains so delightfully undernourished. In the Maritimes, they love to *talk*. (In Newfoundland, they love to drink, but that's another chapter.) Flora MacDonald, telling the story of an ambulance filled with mickeys of rye whiskey (it was, um, election day) and driven by nuns is worthy of Mike Royko and his Chicago ward-heeling and judge-buying epics.

It is clear, listening to these folk, why they are almost always out of power: they delight in talk, while the Grits, who mutter and shrug a lot, get on with the business of shivving their opponents and conniving how to ambush, on a budget vote, a band of innocents who couldn't organize a four-house milk route. It is also clear why Camp has retreated from full-time slavery in the Toronto advertising world to sylvan isolation in New Brunswick: he talks too well for the Big Lemon.

The view from Camp's large, airy house with the triangular roof and the massive double-glazed windows drifts down over the eighty acres to the winter-grey trees and the restless white ice of the lake itching for spring. The apple trees outside the window are brittle and wizened and one fears that the tiny birds, grateful for the March sunshine, will snap their frail branches. In fact, these trees will endure, as will this muddy earth and these people outside Jemseg, above Grand Lake, in the woods-and-water solitude of the lonely land called New Brunswick.

Dalton Camp is the best-known politician-in-exile captive in Canada. While the civil rights people froth and foment about Soviet dissidents deprived of intellectual succor, the Tories' own version of creative starvation sits and crinkles his eyes with laughter and regards the world with expansive bemusement. In a nervous party still infested with cobwebs of anti-intellectualism, he exists as an abandoned resource, somewhat of an imaginative leper, allowed to meet his peers only under cover of darkness, a scarlet lady of the mind.

The reason Camp talks so well, and writes so well, is because of an athletic accident. Although he was born in New Brunswick, he was raised as a boy in California and, because of long hours at basketball in shoes that were too small, developed severe foot problems that put him in bed for nearly a year.

His father, taking advantage of a captive mind, brought him six books a week—the classics of literature. Each week he would return with six more—first giving his son a quiz to make sure he had absorbed the previous six. It was a magnificent opportunity to shape a young mind. Dalton Camp is the only person I have ever met whose brain was formed through his feet.

147

What has happened to Dalton Camp, scarcely a spent force at sixty-three, is illustrative of the sterile quality of Canadian politics in general and the Progressive Conservative Party in particular. (Those of us of Alice-in-Wonderland bent who have for years marvelled at the dichotomy of a party that can be both "progressive" and "conservative" were greatly heartened by Joe Clark's discovery while prime minister of a "deficit" that somehow could be "stimulative." For such small mercies are we grateful.)

The Grits, if they had him, would secret Camp in some spare pad above a Yorkville boutique in trendy Toronto, redolent with Jerry Brown aphorisms and copies of *The Village Voice*. The Tories, secure in their masochism, content to confront the electorate with teen-age versions of John Bracken, consign Dalton Camp to political Coventry, smug in their belief that humour should never sully the earnest intent of the party of losers.

For the Tories, a sense of humour is a handicap, a burden generally left behind when one adopts the litany of conservatism. On Camp's mantel, above the double-faced fireplace that stretches from the expansive sitting room clear through to the dining room, there is a dreadful moustache cup of one John Diefenbaker. Camp, one understands, is a collector of kitsch. It is a work of atrocity committed by a luckily anonymous Victoria artist who thrusts such abominations on Yankee tourists. Camp loves it.

Wallowing in their hot tub of Western Canada, the Clark Tories were afraid to touch the Camp expertise. For one thing, they seemed tremulous about the Maritime Mafia. Camp, of course — despite the overlay of slick Toronto ad-man laid on him by Dief — is a down-homer, the inventor and confidant of Stanfield. He's a New Brunswick apple-picker who has returned to his roots. Flora MacDonald, a Camp protégé, is a Cape Breton product. Fin MacDonald, who was brought into the Clark office too late in its wrigglings to save the leader, is from the same Camp-Stanfield connection.

In all, the Liberals seem more aware than the Tories that the Maritimes' main export is the brain drain. Dalton Camp, because he is too bright and shrewd, because he writes an influential newspaper column — and mainly because he has a Diefenbaker moustache cup over his mantel — is sent to purgatory. His party contains its own self-destruct mechanism.

Like the aborigine who went crazy trying to throw away a boomerang, the Recessive Convertibles can never quite get rid of Camp. The man who did the party the favour of beheading John Diefenbaker has never been forgiven for the merciful deed and large clumps of the faithful would still rather ingest sawdust than acknowledge a handshake from this political leper.

Camp refuses to compromise, a man who does not so much flit on the edges of the party as hover over it, a bald hummingbird with heavy eyelids, a Liberal turned Tory who now operates somewhat as the *deus ex machina* of the New Brunswick underbrush, delivering zots of lightning in his pronouncements and assessments. He is regarded as suspiciously as the party's version of herpes, though half of the constituents don't know what it means and, considering their austere social habits, have little chance of coming within handshake experience of it.

He treats the English language as a precious commodity, to be doled out in carefully balanced segments, a wise old jeweller polishing his gems. In his book *Points of Departure* (from a Karl Marx line: "Individuals always did and always do take themselves as points of departure"), he displays his usual delicate touch. Diefenbaker enters a hotel "like a smoking girandole." Camp spots Iona Campagnolo: "two blue eyelids, resembling lamps on some cruising celestial vehicle." George Hees "possessed a formidable capacity for unconscionable insincerity."

Camp, of course, was an early authority on Joe Clark, the aspirant who once so annoyed him — when the young Albertan worked for him — with his nervous interruptions. Camp found a "fierce discipline" beneath Clark's awkwardness. The key, detected in Clark's days as a student Tory, was that "there was nothing of him in excess." No one had ever seen him drunk. He didn't smoke. He wasn't boisterous or profane.

149

This blandness, this lack of "life's lumps and scars," even led Camp to ask whether there was ever a man who had come to power "with so little tutelage in compassion." (He could think of only one: Trudeau.)

There was a long correspondence between these two men, who were twenty years apart in age, as they plotted — one the president of the party, and the other head of the young Tories — how to get rid of Dief. The letters show the Clark passion for organization and detail but they also show the student politician "least liked the necessity of making a choice — the instinct for collegiality already discernible. He had the makings of a model chairman."

Best of all, when the firestorm over Dief finally broke, Camp suddenly realized that Clark somehow was not involved. He plotted, but then carefully did not get hit with the splatter. Clark, whose whole life was politics, purposely stayed away from the famous and acrimonious annual convention of 1966 when Camp forced the issue, over a furious Diefenbaker, on a leadership review. If you were ever in a fight, says Dalton Camp, "the safest man around to hold your coat would be Clark."

Camp's remarks about the "model chairman" were written in 1979 — after Clark came to power and before he blew it. They proved to be, if meant as a compliment, a perfect description instead of the reason for the fall of the Clark government. Chairmen do not make good leaders, and while the young prime minister delayed calling Parliament for six months, while he fiddled with organization, while he delayed putting the patronage pork barrel in motion, delayed sacking at least a juicy handful of high swivel servants who were covered with Liberal camouflage, the public made a gradual decision that this was not a leader at all they had put into Sussex Drive but an expeditor, a head of a committee — a chairman.

PART THREE

Wizards and Witches

11 East and West

*"The Witches of the East and West were terribly
wicked, and had they not thought I was more
powerful than they themselves, they would surely
have destroyed me. As it was, I lived in deadly fear of
them for many years."*

The Yellow Brick Road fans out across the land, searching
for the woebegone, the disparate, the lost, the lonely, the philo-
sophically confused, those with overloaded psyches and those
with underfed personalities — wherever a Tory might be
found. The Bay Street barons do not control the party (no one
controls the party, which is the problem).

There are Conservatives in Quebec, so few that two of
the party's candidates in the last election finished behind the
Rhinoceros Party. Despite Clark's claim to have raised the
party's support to unprecedented heights in the opinion polls,
he ended with one Quebec MP out of seventy-five, fewer than
Dief, fewer than Stanfield. The lonely stranger is Roch LaSalle,
a mercurial, nervous leaper who flits between having his campaign debts erased by a Mulroney-sponsored fund-raising dinner to ardently supporting Clark. He is not a rock upon which
you would build a church.

There are Conservatives down on the farm in Saskatchewan, suspicious of socialism, wary of Toronto, contemptuous of Ottawa, chary of the French fact. They wear their trac-
tor hats and curl in the winter, waiting for the clean breath of
the Prairie spring so they can put their crops in, aware that the

Natural Governing Party has managed, over its long tenure, to mismanage a transportation system to the extent that they have been instructed not to grow more wheat to feed the hungry world because the railways cannot get it to tidewater.

The monumental feeling of disgust for Ottawa and its minions can only be understood by talking to these men and having it explained that they cannot do fully what they do best, grow wheat, because the genii who run the country cannot get the railways to operate to a 1983 level. We will not go into The Crow. There is enough humour in the world (much of it contained within the Liberal cabinet).

It is generally forgotten that the Tories, supposedly the party of Bay Street, in fact have found four of their leaders — and three of their prime ministers — on the Prairies. The Tories, in truth, are a party of stubborn individualists (as opposed to the slick, Daley-like grease of the Liberals) and John Bracken, Arthur Meighen, R. B. Bennett and John Diefenbaker were undoubtedly, in their day, as uncomfortable-appearing as Joe Clark is.

There are Conservatives, nothing but Conservatives, in once-almighty Alberta, now living on its Heritage Fund, digging up the jam jars in the back garden and spending the mouldy bills. If Alberta does not have its previous clout, it can still reach across the nation and help elect an Irish Catholic from Montreal rather than a kid from High River who cannot ride a horse and so is suspect.

The threat that Prince Peter Lougheed might unleash his forces if Bill Davis attempted to ride into the Tory race was formidable and would have divided this divisive party even more, full as it is of bullet holes and axe wounds, great tears and rents. Davis knew it and Davis pulled back. Tory meets Tory. Tory dislikes Tory. It is what keeps the Liberals strong.

There are kooky Conservatives in Lotusland, hunkered down in The Village on the Edge of the Rain Forest, going under the name of Social Credit — which is neither social or gives credit. They make up the eighth Conservative province in the land, the others being Alberta, Saskatchewan, Ontario, New Brunswick, Nova Scotia, Prince Edward Island and Newfoundland. Only Manitoba's social democrats and Quebec's watered-down separatists are outside the fold.

Provincially, Canada is Tory. It is when the party tries to step up into a higher league that it runs into difficulties on The Yellow Brick Road.

British Columbians, one must understand, view all other residents of Canada with an attitude of intolerant puzzlement. Anyone so stupid as not to live in Narcissus-of-the-Pacific absolutely deserves the lousy weather elsewhere. The vaster forms of contempt are reserved, of course, for Ontario, the fading linchpin of Confederation, where all the bucks are siphoned and where, inside every office clerk, is a Conrad Black struggling to get out.

When a proper Torontonian male is nose-deep in paperwork at 5:30 PM quitting time, eager to earn the company bonus that will give him a swimming pool shaped like his ulcer, his British California equivalent is long gone into the hot tub, doing underwater research with his secretary on the specific gravity of gin.

It was with some astonishment, therefore, that a reporter discovered the remarkable invasion in 1981 of the inner circles of the B.C. government by a clutch of Ontario Tories, complete with pinstripe suits and bumps on their knobbly foreheads that are meant to indicate intelligence and organizational guile. It was not so much an invasion, really, as a recruitment — a Lend-Lease program equivalent to the Marshall Plan, which rebuilt Europe after the war.

The Big Blue Machine, for interesting and the usual devious reasons, was trying to resurrect the fading reputation of MiniWac, the one and only premier of Disneyland-with-Mountains, Bill Bennett. If the socialist horde is beating at the gate — with capitalism in peril — who better to come riding to the rescue but Brampton Billy Davis, the man who has managed to reduce Canada's most powerful province to a parish pump? Who better indeed?

What was happening was that Bennett and Social Credit had been so low in the polls and public esteem in the past year that NDP leader Dave Barrett hadn't had to open his yap

in public except to yawn. It was the considered wisdom over the double-breasted Scotches in the Vancouver Club and in the tobacco-stained pubs where journalists hang out that the Socreds were dead.

So Bennett, who doesn't know many people (when you're in a hurry to make a million dollars you don't stop to shake hands much), went back to his hometown Kelowna roots to dragoon a small-business friend, one Hugh Harris, a taciturn type who had a broken nose, a pipe and a tin suitcase. Over the next year, this wandering scribe kept bumping into him in the strangest of places — Ottawa dark corners, the shadows of the Empire Club, the speaking podium in the Royal York in Toronto where the elite meet to greet and gripe about the terrible state of affairs since women were given the vote.

Hugh Harris, before his tragic death of a brain tumour, travelled about the continent for a good two years, studying political organizations elsewhere, going to U.S. presidential conventions — assigned by the granitically determined Mini-Wac to neutralize the famed constituency spadework of the most militant NDP movement in Canada.

All of a sudden, there are quiet announcements. Patrick Kinsella, the guru who had given Bill Davis (finally) his majority government in Ontario, is leaving Ontario to take charge — though no one will admit it — of the political organization of the woolhats, mouth-breathers, anti-vivisectionists and jumped-up used car salesmen of the Social Credit funny-money troop.

This is the man who turned down the entreaties of Joe Clark to replace Paul Curley as head of the Progressive Conservative headquarters in Ottawa. Why would Buttermilk Bill release his right arm to the kooks and strip miners? Read on.

Next thing we hear is that Dr. Norman Spector, another recruit from Ontario, has been brought in at the assistant deputy minister level to be in charge of Bennett's office, a scene of some past confusion. He is, at this stage, just thirty-two and presumably has some beans, aside from a special gift for being a mole — early detected — among press types so as to rat back to his boss. Next to emigrate is Jerry Lampert, a political science graduate, Bill Davis' man in eastern Ontario who was in charge of nineteen constituencies there, finger-lickin' Tory-pluckin' land. He used to brief Joe Clark and was campaign manager in Ottawa for Jean Pigott.

Coming on the scene was Bruce Lane, a dignified wagon master (i.e., don't lose the luggage and lean on the press) for both Davis and Clark. There was someone called Dave Tkachuk, executive director of the Saskatchewan Tories, scheduled to become another of Bennett's boat people, dedicated to pouring burning oil and polls on the rapidly regrouping NDP.

Now why, one might ask, was the juggernaut of the Ontario Tory boredom factor being unleashed on the laid-back electorate of helpless B.C.? As a result of the latest Davis election win, which has stretched Ontario Conservative rule past forty years, both Liberal leader Stuart Smith and NDP head Michael Cassidy gave up and resigned.

With Tory premier Sterling Lyon, with his Reaganomics, headed for inevitable defeat in Manitoba to the wretched socialists, there was the natural free-enterprise fear (Allan Blakeney's NDP still then supposedly secure in Saskatchewan) that poor Peter Lougheed was going to be left a lone capitalist in a Western Canadian sea of socialism — as he was in the middle 1970s.

Brampton Billy, with ineffectual Clark increasingly isolated within his own caucus, could certainly use a power base in the third-largest province in the eventuality that he would decide to go for the Tory bundle in Ottawa.

Could the forces of free enterprise — emboldened by the odd couple of Maggie Thatcher and Ronnie Reagan — swallow a match between the Big Blue Machine and the disciples of the A + B Theorem? Was there a capitalist conspiracy going on? Bet your sweet bippy.

Now we have MiniWac, emboldened by the two per cent shift in the popular vote that gave him an increased mandate in the spring of 1983, out in hot pursuit of Ronnie and Maggie, attempting to establish new beachheads in dynamic cost-cutting. Battered wives are shoved aside, homeless children are passed by, human rights considerations are stepped over, the snivel servants must be slashed by ten thousand jobs, B.C. must lead the way for the nation in roughshod government.

And who showed up at the federal Conservative leadership convention, their noses pressed against the glass? Such pseudo-Socreds (Tories) as B.C. cabinet ministers Stephen Rogers and Brian Smith. They are among a number of eager political transvestites who attempted to arrange legitimate accreditation as delegates. Among those wanting such an arrangement was a new Socred backbencher, a man who, while he was an MP, distinguished himself.

There are, at appropriate intervals, paeans of praise heaped upon certain individuals in Ottawa who are deemed the epitome of all that parliamentary tradition stands for. Whether it is Ged Baldwin or Gordon Fairweather or perhaps Stanley Knowles, the encyclopedias are hauled out to amass all the sterling qualities encompassed in an MP who is an adornment to the calling. There are a few paragons and they deserve to be recognized.

Missing, however, is a compilation of the bad MPs, the true incompetents who in their own way have perfected the art of *how* to be an absolutely callow politician. I have a candidate, a man I will hold up and defend to the death as the nominee for the worst Member of Parliament of the decade. Voters, I give you handsome John Reynolds, the one-edition wonder, now residing in the B.C. Legislature! Behind the tinsel, here's the real tinsel.

Who else had *Hansard* crammed with questions on air mattresses, the polar-bear protection bill, fire-extinguishing foam and Pierre Trudeau's car? Who ran the earliest and most disastrous 1976 campaign for the Tory leadership? Who conducted a one-man campaign to bring back hanging and may have blundered into starting a prison riot? Who dares doubt my choice as the title-holder, over the last decade, as Worst MP in Ottawa?

The surprising thing about the man chosen for the honour is the direction he took. He was an energetic thirty when first elected in 1972. His British Columbia constituency of

Burnaby-Richmond-Delta had the largest number of voters (eighty-one thousand) of any riding in Western Canada at the time. In 1974 he had the highest winning majority of any MP elected in B.C. He seemed to have everything going his way.

Reynolds instead chose the low road, the shallow route, the hot-line philosophy of life. There are giants of Parliament Hill and there are Lilliputians. John Reynolds was from Lilliput.

He was as could be expected, a salesman—born in Toronto but raised in Montreal where highschool didn't prove as enticing as a sales career at Woolsworth's. Later he was with, appropriately, Rust Craft greeting cards and then with something called Ethicon Structures.

He spent time in San Francisco and still brandishes that brash American self-advertisement glitter that made him appear so strange in double-breasted Ottawa. He was all trendy sideburns and rakish good looks, somewhat resembling a faro dealer on a Mississippi paddle wheeler. He fitted his riding, a southern slice of Vancouver that displays all the acne of suburban growth — all that restless ranch-house ambition and wife-swapping, curling-club, credit-card confusion. John got his name in the headlines, and aren't headlines what politics is all about?

He had the attention span of a hummingbird. Disapproving press critics would attempt to zero in on one of his spurious issues only to find he had fled the subject, flitting off to yet another one-day cause. Mary Steinhauser, a social worker who had befriended prisoners, is killed by point-blank shots from guards in a hostage-taking in a B.C. penitentiary. Reynolds in far-off Ottawa suddenly has evidence that fifteen hostages were forced to drink "massive doses" of a hypnotic drug. How does he know? He can't say. Documentation? Whoops, it's tomorrow's paper and another issue.

Howard Hughes in the news? Reynolds is suddenly the champion of a shady Hughes aide, John Meier, who is living in his riding and claims the CIA is spying on him. The RCMP waste three weeks looking for the alleged "spy" and conclude the whole thing may be a hoax. Four years later, the U.S. asks

160

for extradition for Meier, who is wanted on conspiracy-to-murder charges.

Wherever there is a faint sniff of prejudice, Reynolds was there in a sprint, like a boar rooting out truffles. The thought of a French TV station in Vancouver (then the only link missing the national network), of course, inflamed the Reynolds psyche. He took ads in the Vancouver papers, collected eighteen thousand signatures against the station and was prominent at the CRTC hearings, sideburns aquiver in his Cause for a Day.

Hanging? The decision of the House of Commons, acting like all civilized nations, was not enough. Reynolds urged a national referendum on the non-issue (at a time when all parties in the House, his own included, were trying to cool René Lévesque's brave plans for a referendum on separation). Veteran journalists believed that Reynolds, by barging into the tense situation at the B.C. Penitentiary, may have accidentally triggered a 1979 riot that caused one million dollars damage.

The most hilarious incident in the career of this overreacher was when he viewed himself as a future prime minister. The TV cameras were still warm on the night Robert Stanfield lost the 1974 election and Reynolds was announcing that the party needed a new leader, one more of the right wing. His sentiments may have been connected with the fact that Stanfield, no fan of the Reynolds' Woolworth's brashness, kept him so far distant in the backbenches that his styled coiffure brushed the curtains and he almost suffered a severe attack of moths.

At any rate, early in 1975 — more than a year before Stanfield was to step down — Reynolds became the first candidate in the field, announcing a one-hundred-dollars-a-plate fund-raising dinner for himself in the Hotel Vancouver, chaired by a crusty Australian sea captain turned distiller and a former hanging judge. When the one thousand putative guests turned out to be some thirty, the dinner was aborted and Canada lost another immortal at 24 Sussex Drive.

There were further embarrassments. There was, for in-

161

stance, that curious trip to Washington State to meet Senator Scoop Jackson, when Reynolds pledged to support any retaliatory legislation against Ottawa's Bill C-58, which ended tax concessions for Canadian firms advertising in the United States. Noting the Reynolds' quote that "most Canadians would support any American moves to straighten out our government," the *Victoria Times* sardonically nominated him for patriot of the year.

Handsome John, in fact, may be ideal for modern politics. He has no shame. It is impossible to insult him because he is already headed off gleefully to the next spurious issue, good for at least two radio clips and the street edition. Maybe there is, within the political system, a basic need to have men of shallow persuasion bouncing across the surface of public affairs like a skipping stone. The next time you hear all those service-club speakers ramble on about the giants, think of the Lilliputians.

Maclean's magazine said, "In the world of politics, one man stands head and shoulders below the rest — John Reynolds." When I initially detailed many of the above activities, it was the first (and I believe only) time that Joe Clark, then prime minister, ever complimented me about anything. Reynolds was then a member of his caucus.

Once Clark's views on him became apparent, Reynolds resigned to move to two higher callings, first as an open-mouth host on a Vancouver radio station and then into the food franchise business (hamburger, meet hamburger), and hence, into the mining market, where he became wealthy. He invested in a better tailor and acquired, along with more expensive shoes, a dignified tinge of white to his temples, and tinted shades that made him look like a minor league Hollywood star.

On three days' notice, before the 1983 British Columbia election, he launched a surprise assault on the Social Credit nomination for West Vancouver, the Martini Mountain riding of Lotusland where those who do not have swimming pools on their yachts can usually fit their yachts into their swimming pools.

The Socreds, of course, are merely the B.C. version of the

Tories, a populist mish-mash of evangelists, chiropractors, lawn mower salesmen and cold-eyed money men. The cold-eyed money man who fuelled the Reynolds ambush was Murray Pezim, a flamboyant stock promoter who lives a life that would be rejected in a Damon Runyon tale as a trifle too garish.

Son of a Toronto butcher, "The Pez" arrived in the wide-open Vancouver penny mines market more than a decade ago with partner Earl Glick, both of them taking their alligator-weave shoes west to the relief of the Toronto Stock Exchange, which did not share their approach to life, love or their pursuit of confused but financially secure widows. On Howe Street, home of the Vancouver Stock Exchange, Pezim and Glick were punned as Sleazy and Slick.

The Pez, when he is not in trouble with regulatory authorities, casually makes and loses fortunes. He once went broke by bankrolling a heavyweight fight in Vancouver between Muhammad Ali and the ponderous if brave Canadian George Chuvalo, whose face was sliced into mince-meat by an elegant Ali with the distraction of a man with a rapier carving up a cauliflower.

Pezim is now riding high again, controlling some fifty-seven resource-based firms listed on the VSE, delighting over the fact that he has zapped his TSE tormentors by grabbing the main part of the action in the recent heavy gold findings in northern Ontario's Hemlo field. He threw a flurry into that stalled "people's capitalism" giant, the British Columbia Resources Investment Corporation, by buying $3.1 million worth of BCRIC shares in a well-publicized attempt to gain control.

He has his own press agent, amuses himself by flying in people like Milton Berle and other Hollywood golden oldies for benefit roasts for his friends, and sprinkles champagne and cigars behind him like Oral Roberts moving through a crowd of supplicants.

The Pez and his crowd of hustlers, packing the meeting, snatched the Socred nomination for Reynolds in the safe seat, and the tall Tory-turned-hotliner-turned-franchise-king-

163

turned-Socred has now been placed firmly in the backbench in Victoria by MiniWac, Premier Bill Bennett, who knows bug-eyed ambition when he sees it.

Watching all this with some amusement and narrowed eyes was the unlikely overseer of the Howe Street action, the Socreds' chief bagman, who wants to succeed Bennett as head of the party, and premier. He is Peter Brown, a former naughty actor in the stock market who is now the president of the VSE, a refugee from *The Great Gatsby* who creates new legends about himself at each Saturday-night party.

He is yet another example of this weakness that plagues the Conservative Party: out-riders galloping down the hills at crucial moments can overwhelm the weak federal structure. (It's why "outsider" Mulroney, carefully avoiding the ballot box all these years, was able by a stealthily planned strategy to capture the leadership from all the caucus candidates — a remarkable feat when you consider it carefully.)

Brown, from an establishment family (his brother, Alan, is headmaster at St. George's, *the* private school for boys), has spent most of his life being outrageous. While failing to get a degree at the University of B.C. (he flunked his freshman year three times), he ended a hard-drinking party at his trendy coach house on prestigious Southwest Marine Drive with a tree-felling contest. One tree crashed to earth athwart the prized flower beds of neighbour Frank McMahon, the oil and gas tycoon. By noon the next day McMahon was on his doorstep: "I want you off the property by tomorrow. I've just bought this place."

The Rabbit, as he is known, was dazzling a young lady, an aide to Senator Jack Austin, at a lunch at L'Orangerie, a Vancouver restaurant with a sliding glass roof that he helped to finance, when he noticed her Timex watch. "Let's see if the ads work," he said, removing her watch and dropping it into her glass of Dom Perignon, which he uses regularly as mouthwash. The watch failed the test so The Rabbit summoned the chauffeur waiting outside in his Rolls Corniche (brown in colour, naturally), who had to drive off to purchase another watch and have it back on the lady's hand in thirty minutes. This is the way we keep the socialist hordes at bay.

One of Brown's party tricks, after downing his champagne, is to eat the glass. He owns seventy pairs of identical Gucci loafers. At forty-one, he is worth about ten million dollars and boasts that he has made two dozen of his salesmen in his Canarim investment house into millionaires. He is now opening branches in Geneva and London. He also collects the boodle that keeps MiniWac's Socred machine functioning and — like Mulroney — thinks he can somehow parachute in at the proper time and take over from Bennett.

This is what keeps the national Conservative movement so sporadic and feeble-witted at election time, up against the constant pressure of the Grits. The Tories are filled with opportunists like Brown, like Reynolds, like their Toronto counterparts, who want to dabble when the stakes are high but who do not put in homework overtime. The Liberals are professionals at politics. The Tories are still amateurs.

Some of them live in Saskatchewan.

In mid-July, after a soaking rain, the thrusting grain waves green and strong across the flatlands fifty miles south of Regina. In the hall at Rouleau, the three-piece band wears white shoes, red satin shirts and black vests.

The occasion is a coming together of the glue that keeps this country together, the glue being the concentric circles of family strengths that bind and stick. It is a family reunion of three generations that were nurtured in the navel of the country, the wheat belt of Saskatchewan, the prime example that blood does run thicker than water — or grasshoppers or hail or Depression relief lines.

Families' ties are stronger than armies' and fraternities' and clubs' and councils' and parliaments'. Forged through the ineluctable experience of Saskatchewan in the Dirty Thirties, they stick like warts.

This reunion — forty-two grandchildren, fifty-five great-grandchildren—is what is left of the heritage of John E. Clarke. Born September 21, 1880. Died 1956. His seed is sprinkled across the land. There is Dora, born 1906. Then Irene, Edna, then a daughter who died, then Leslie, Ruby, Jack, Lloyd,

Harvey, Dick, Jim and finally Dale, who was born in 1931. Mary Ethel Clarke, born July 12, 1885, died 1964, raised children for forty years on her husband's farm outside Hearne, southwest of Rouleau.

The Cactus Hills are to the west, the Dirt Hills to the south, the Big Muddy Badlands next to the North Dakota border. There was, on the Clarke farm forty years ago, a windmill that drew water from a well for the horse trough — nearly a half-century before the energy-panicky world decided that harnessing the wind may be one of the solutions after all.

There are, in the preliminary layer, sons and daughters from Georgia, Ottawa and British Columbia. There are farmers still on the original family soil, optometrists, nurses, teachers, artists.

On the second layer — their children — there are engineers, veterinarians, RCMP officers, school superintendents, social workers, dental assistants. The final layer down, there are personnel officers and students and babes — all victims of the cultural stickum to the sources.

There was, on one side, the Webbs, from Bromyard, Herefordshire, supposedly related to the Webbs, Sidney and Beatrice, of Fabian socialist fame. James Webb, one of the first settlers in Saskatchewan, lived in a sod house just west of Rouleau when the tall, untamed prairie grass was such a threat that uncontrollable fires swept through it. He plowed the open prairie with a team of oxen. Today, I note with great surprise and delight, his heirs sit in forty-thousand-dollar tractors and listen — their CB rigs on hold — in air-conditioned comfort to music coming from a CBC studio in Toronto.

The Clarkes have that square, stubborn face that reveals they are from Northern Ireland. Surviving a shipwreck off Newfoundland, they made it to the Ottawa Valley, then homesteading in Saskatchewan. John Clarke came from a family of fifteen.

He arrived in Rouleau in 1898, went into the livery business, was a councillor for the first municipality (his province until 1905 was still part of the Northwest Territories).

166

He was a longtime reeve, a manager of soccer, baseball and hockey clubs (Ken Doherty went on to the Maple Leafs), a chairman of the school board, and a stout Tory voter most of his life.

Ethel Clarke was a pillar of the Women's Christian Temperance Union. John Clarke and his seven sons, on special occasions, had a bottle of rye in the barn. It never got further than the barn. The WCTU ruled the house.

There is, on this reunion weekend, a pilgrimage to a Sunday afternoon picnic nestled beneath ground-level heat in a leafy ravine outside Avonlea. It was Avonlea that spawned the famous four Campbell curling brothers, ten times winner of the Brier.

The pickles, as always at any Prairie table, predominate. There are three twenty-five-pound roasts of beef, barbecued in two bisected oil drums. The recipe is simple: add lemons, twelve onions, twenty bay leaves, thirty cloves, two gallons water, one gallon wine, sixty peppercorns, ten tablespoons sugar, ten of salt, four teaspoons ginger, smoke chips. Plus an acre of pickles.

It is, as it happens, a full moon. The banjo comes out, and the guitar, then the saxophone. Whey-faced six-year-olds, exhausted from dancing till midnight the evening before with adults who do not deprive children of adult fun, collapse facedown on blankets beneath the trees. The farm wives, greeting or departing, kiss you full on the lips in contrast to the tentative city custom of nervous side-long swipes at the cheek. The moon rises, the saxophone wails.

It is not quite the same as Depression days when the stud-hero of the one-room schoolhouse wheeled his pinto pony stallion into the barn, as much the BMOC as today's greaser with his muscle car peeling rubber. It's hard to imagine anyone now spending his recess time snaring gophers by the neck with binder twine as they emerged sputtering and indignant from their drowned-out burrows.

The heirs of John Clarke, while their wheat goes to China, Bangladesh and beyond, drive enormous machines that seem like moon vehicles — huge campers, gigantic ambulatory

167

homes that take them to Florida to flee the dreary winter. They have, with their prosperity, insulated themselves from their past, which may have seemed romantic to us but is merely a nuisance for them. It was character building, in that there was a lot of banjo playing, but no one would offer to duplicate the experience.

I have some small personal interest in John E. Clarke. He was my grandfather.

12 The Land of Buttermilk and Money

"In this country everyone must pay for everything he gets."

It must be understood that Dr. Foth regards the Forward-Backwards Party as a patient in need, rather like someone requiring a transfusion. I am, I blush while admitting it, the journalistic equivalent of the Red Cross. As the 1975 inventor of The Candidate from Whimsy, Brian Mulroney, I thought it only fair in 1983 to help my fellow Prairie small-town boy, Joe Maybe.

In the March 21 1983 edition of *Maclean's,* I submitted the incontrovertible truth that there were really only two candidates in the leadership race: Clark and Mulroney. When you come to think about it, there were only two men who had prepared themselves properly for the role of future prime minister — Mulroney learning his French in the street fights of Baie Comeau, Clark painfully and persistently learning his on trips to Europe, then by shrewdly marrying an ambitious wife who grew up with the language. (It was Keith Spicer, the first Commissioner of Official Language — and last witty Ottawa mandarin — who advised, accurately, that the best way to learn French was in bed. He has recently married a Swiss lady. We await the results. I digress.)

I pointed out in this watershed column that Bill Davis was, in reality, a regional candidate, viewed as such in the rest of the country because he has never taken the time to cast himself in a national image, let alone attempt a passing knowledge of French in a lifetime of aspiring to high political office. (Davis is such a small-town boy that he has his chauffeur drive him, practically every evening, back to his home in downtown Brampton, for fear he will be corrupted by the alien atmosphere of the Big Lemon, Toronto.)

On March 25, on a Montreal radio open-line show, Joe Clark allowed that Davis, if he entered the leadership race, would be regarded as "a regional candidate." His case was not helped by the Toronto *Star*, in a headline on his comments, stating: DAVIS INEXPERIENCED CLARK SAYS.

The fury in the Big Blue Machine was unabated. Their operatives regarded Clark as peanut butter unalloyed, but their chief — while tanning himself in Florida during Clark's plaintive suicide in 1980 — had been muttering unenthusiastically all along that Clark was his choice as leader. The "regional" comment finished that.

A senior aide to Clark was asked later what had happened to the anonymous aide who had advised his man to offer the description of the Ontario leader on the Montreal radio show.

"Too bad," the Clarkian man advised. "Nice young man. He would have been thirty-four tomorrow."

It is not, I submit, my responsibility for the ultimate outcome of my free advice to those seeking the prime minister's throne. Brian Mulroney took the good doctor's counsel and ran, the Tory party taking seven years to accept the wisdom of the intelligence. Pierre Elliott Himself, with who-can-say what dire results, has never, in his fifteen years, such is the evidence of history, accepted my many urgings. If Joe Clark, in a fit of headstrong abandon, seizes upon one of my theories, surely the burden of blame should not rest on these frail shoulders. The defence rests.

Joe Clark, whether he lifted the notion or not, was, however correct in labelling Davis as a "regional candidate." Western Canada dislikes him, for rational reasons (his benign neglect of Clark in the 1980 loss, his anti-Alberta stance on energy) and for the usual irrational ones (anyone tainted with the brush of Toronto obviously must be deeply flawed).

170

Quebec had no time for Davis (who in truth is a regional politician *within* a region). His cherished links with small-town Brampton — while sustaining in him the links to the seed of Ontario Toryism — have made him a smaller man in the Canadian perspective. He dissipated — unconsciously, because of his chauvinism — the Confederation linchpin role with Quebec that his predecessor, the admirable John Robarts, so nurtured.

When one considers it, it is unconscionable that the premier of the largest and richest province in Canada, cheek-and-jowl with Quebec, could with an unknowing contempt reach the age of fifty-three without even attempting a Mickey Mouse Berlitz command of a few French phrases. One has only to put oneself into the mental apparatus of the thoughtful Québécois to know what that indicates.

The suspiciously timed announcement of the Davis government that it would put into full legislative vigour the missing parts of the rights for francophones merely added to the Quebec cynicism about Davis. Ontario suddenly announced it would extend the rights for an education in French to all francophones, regardless of numbers. Manitoba, with its small francophone population, by court order conforms to the new constitution. New Brunswick, acknowledging its Acadian minority, has voluntarily extended those rights.

Ontario, with its five hundred thousand francophones comprising the largest French-speaking community outside Quebec, has procrastinated on giving to them the same rights that anglophones enjoy in Quebec — until Davis's *coitus interruptus* leadership dance. The announcement from Queen's Park that Bill had given the okay to full provisions of the constitution only confirmed the feelings of Quebec intellectuals — not to mention the even more jaundiced residents of the taverns — that Buttermilk Billy was trying to feather his leadership nest.

The man behind the omnipresent grin is the most cautious of men. He commissioned forty-eight polls before announcing the date of his last provincial election. Canadian Facts, a Toronto market research firm, was hired in mid-March to do a poll on Davis's national strength. A month later, the results were leaked to the Toronto *Star*. They showed that Davis would do better than Clark in a federal election against either Pierre Trudeau or John Turner. An unleaked part of the poll revealed that support for Davis was soft among Conservative Party members.

The Atlantic provinces? Hatfield would have supported him — courted support for him in his usual avalanche of late-night phone calls — but the rest of that neglected area of the world was decidedly soft. (If Western Canada is rigidly hostile to Toronto and Ontario, the gentle Atlantic people regard it as a Me Generation version of Sodom and Gomorrah, filled with people who probably kiss other men's wives on greeting them at cocktail parties.)

Bill Davis didn't run, quite simply, because the numbers weren't there. Has he ever lost an election in his life? No. How would he know how to deal with losing? No one knew. Some worried. Eddie Goodman advised Davis not to run because, according to Hugh Segal, "Eddie didn't want the premier to get hurt. Eddie worried much more than Norm Atkins and me about how well Mr. Davis would bounce back if he lost."

An intimate provides an insight. He suggests that, after three months of agonizing, Bill Davis made up his mind not to run as he was standing on a stepladder with a paintbrush in his hand. He was helping his son Neal fix up his house in Brampton. "I really think that's when it happened," said this close friend. "When he was standing there, brush in hand, grubby clothes, and a paint-speckled pipe in his mouth. I think that's when he realized what he would be giving up."

I think not. Bill Davis made his decision, as do most current politicians, on the basis of what our modern alchemists, the pollsters, tell them. The entrails on the floor, stirred through a computer, told his boffins that it was not a certainty he would win. Surely it wasn't worth giving up the perks of power of running the most important province of the Great White North which, as we know, is made up almost exclusively of hockey and bingo players.

172

The hot-shot salesman is called into the supervisor's office, to be told that his billings are so tremendous that he is being given a promotion, posted to Sudbury. "Sudbury?" the hot-shot exclaims. "That's a promotion? The only things that come out of Sudbury are hockey players and hookers." "My wife," shouts the supervisor, "comes from Sudbury!" "Yeah?" says the salesman. "What position does she play?" I digress.

Whatever the reasons why Davis made his decision, the rest of the country had reason to be grateful.

(It is never mentioned in print, but often at dinner parties, that religion is still a major factor — in politics in Ontario the last refuge in Canada where, if you can believe it, the Orange Lodge still holds a King Billy parade in downtown Toronto each July 12. The provincial NDP, under the leadership of the brilliant Stephen Lewis, from a Jewish family — son of the late David Lewis, leader of the federal NDP — reached Opposition status. His religion was never discussed in print, only talked about in private.

(Former Ontario Liberal leader Stuart Smith, by way of his Hamilton psychiatry practice, was out of the Montreal Jewish community, in fact was trying for the federal Liberal nomination in Mount Royal in 1965 when he was suddenly shunted aside for a newcomer by the name of Pierre Elliott Trudeau. When the Ontario whispering campaign, among other things, did him in, he was fixed up as head of the Science Council of Canada, at $92,000 a year, by the government headed by Pierre Elliott Trudeau.

(The most ambitious aspirant to Premier Bill Davis's burnished crown is the bustling Larry Grossman, given in the latest cabinet shuffle the prime portfolio of provincial treasurer. He is clever, hard-working and very ambitious. The smart money around the Toronto dinner parties is that he will never make it against such rivals as Roy McMurtry (if he does not go federal), Dennis Timbrell, the De Gaulle-ish Darcy McKeough and, possibly, Julian Porter. Not because of

Grossman's abilities, but because Ontario would never accept a Jew as premier.

(When Dave Barrett was elected premier of British Columbia, the press — which has never once mentioned his religion in the election campaign — grew very ebullient about the fact that Barrett was the first "Jewish" premier in Canadian political history. The *Globe and Mail*, in an editorial, said that Mr. Barrett was "of the Jewish faith." Pierre Berton wrote a searing letter to the paper asking, "What is wrong with the word Jew? Hitler tried to turn the word Jew into an epithet. I had the feeling that he had failed abysmally. But a few more cop-out phrases like this one and some of your readers will get the feeling that you find something wrong in calling a Jew a Jew. There isn't.")

Similar selfless acts of charitable men occasionally illuminate the nation. Such an act came when Nelson Skalbania, the famed philanthropist, decided to remove himself and his leaky wallet from the Montreal sporting scene he so graced. Another example would be Harold Ballard, the well-known patriot, in determining that he would not move the Hamilton Tiger-Cats into their natural habitat, Varsity Stadium in Toronto. In future years, greying historians will accord them great significance for their contributions to national unity.

In the same way, Bill Davis of downtown Brampton will be thanked for generations to come for his magnanimous decision not to lead the Recessive Convertible Party to victory in the next election. By doing so, by tugging on his forelock and shyly backing away at the brink of fame, the premier of mighty Ontario has demonstrated something he has never displayed in his term of office — a concern for the country as a whole.

Buttermilk Billy's candidacy — so pushed by his acolytes Norm Atkins and Hugh Segal in the Dalton Camp ad agency (Camp being stuck with Clark) who lusted to run Ottawa, and by all his key ministers, who wanted his job — would have done a number of things.

Just at a time when the incredibly self-destructive Tories had fumbled their way to a fifty-two-per-cent approval by the Canadian electorate, it would have induced internecine regional blood-letting, causing Prince Peter Lougheed (who has good reason to be livid over turncoat-Davis's cynical leaping into bed with Trudeau over the Crosbie eighteen-cent gas budget) to turn his formidable Alberta legislative juggernaut against Davis.

The only province in Canada so monolithic in its political philosophy as to have every single MP from the same party would have mounted a ferocious Western Canada campaign against the slick manipulators of the Big Blue Machine (who had already, as we have seen, planted a base operation in B.C.).

The bullying Pierre Trudeau plan for unilateral constitutional patriation was killed off by Joe Clark with the support of the provinces, which are mostly controlled by Conservative premiers. The only Tory premier who snuggled in with Trudeau was Bill Davis. That has never been, and will never be, forgotten by thoughtful P.C. delegates in the hinterland who do not need elephantine memories to remember treachery that goes under the guise of expediency.

The Grit candidate in the next general election will be, most probably, Toronto's John Turner. To make Toronto's Bill Davis his Tory opponent would have destroyed most every advantage the Conservative party has been building over the past half-dozen years. Bill Davis, with his Queen's Park slickers and ad agency hucksters, would have obliterated the growing belief in the country that it is indeed a time for change. Fifteen years of hollow-based charisma could not really be wiped out by another version of power-tripping.

What really motivated the people pushing Davis to go for Ottawa was conceit, a lofty irritation that the control of their party had kept wafting out of their reach ever since George Drew (everybody's father knew him). If the levers of power were not emanating from Prince Albert they were in Halifax or, for God's sake, in *High River.* The heavy hitters from Toronto could not stand the inherent insult that the city that has a grip on the short hairs of the nation in the key financial and communications areas does not — for some inexplicable reason — also pull the strings of a puppet who could sit on Sussex Drive.

(Does New York, which occupies approximately the same

privileged position in the U.S., whine and moan that presidents seem to come from Georgia, from Michigan, from Missouri? Probably.)

By staying out of the race, Davis left Tory delegates with a truly Canadian choice. By removing the Toronto money and the Toronto clout and the Toronto lust for power, the Davis withdrawal gave the convention an honest choice.

The party the public so wants to elect had before it, if it so chose, the maturing kid from High River who pleaded for a second chance on the grounds that he had grown up at last. He was honest, he was sincere, and he (unlike Bill Davis) had struggled with a wooden Alberta tongue to learn French.

The party had, as its choice, the best mind of all these egos, John Crosbie, gold medallist at two universities, confident, charming, witty — and unilingual, as are most Canadians.

The party could contemplate in its wisdom the fact that if it had failed since Sir John A. because it had never broken into Quebec, it now had a candidate, in Brian Mulroney, who could likely win a dozen or so Quebec seats first time around, the best chance it has had for decades to reconcile the two solitudes.

It was a tough choice. But a fair one. Thank you, Bill Davis. You weren't needed.

PART FOUR

In Search of a Chin

13 The Goofies

"Now there is Mr. Joker, one of our clowns,"
continued the china lady, "who is always trying to
stand upon his head. He has broken himself so often
that he is mended in a hundred places and doesn't
look at all pretty."

The Conservatives at play keep the nation amused. Now that the Toronto Argonauts have become respectable, bored Canadians looking for titillation need only wait for a Tory leadership convention and it all unfolds like the late-night rerun of a silent movie, the Marx Brothers spending an evening at the opera, Mack Sennett throwing cream pies, Buster Keaton being run down by a train, Harold Lloyd dangling from a window of a skyscraper, Laurel and Hardy bumping into each other, Abbott and Costello trying to figure out who's on first. These are the Tories in their search for democracy and we get it all for free.

You couldn't make it up, really. The latest comedy of errors took seven years for the full goofiness of it to unfold. Joe Clark was elected by accident, sort of, in 1976 because law-and-order Claude Wagner had been damaged by his lack of truth about this $300,000 slush fund, the details leaked by the backers of Brian Mulroney, *they* knowing the details because Mulroney was in on the deal in the first place. Could we have made it up?

Clark, stumbling along in the middle of his recalcitrant, surly caucus — resembling, for most of his time as leader, a man walking in molasses, the stickum slowing his progress at every turn — is pushed into a leadership review in 1981 and manages to get an unenthusiastic 66.7 per cent approval. It is what is known as a squatting ovation.

With the click of the knives and the mutterings behind the curtains ever discernible, even while the party has the approval of more than fifty per cent of Canadians in the polls, Winnipeg in frigid January is chosen as a second test of his popularity.

After working the land for two years, wooing delegates, drinking enough coffee in church basements to rust the pipes in a freighter, the leader who had only to survive to become most probably the next prime minister could manage only 66.9 per cent backing. One would think that anyone who, after working hard for two solid years, could increase his popularity by only one-fifth of a percentage point, would take the hint and take up a more satisfying brand of work.

No. Clark, if nothing else, is obstinate. He is, in his own way, as stubborn as his original hero, Mr. Diefenbunker. As Dalton Camp says, Clark has no vanity, but he does have an ego.

The ego wounded, one does not sleep on it, to consider the implications of the Winnipeg vote, to consult with all possible before doing something rash. Instead, the wounded ego, with all of fifty minutes for thought once the vote is announced, declares with some bravado that he will resign forthwith and face his tormentors at a full leadership convention.

It is insane folly, a man not only tripping but then falling on his own sword. Having shot himself in the foot, he then aims slightly higher. Harold Lloyd would have looked on with admiration. Buster Keaton might even have managed a smile at the magnificence of the bad judgment. A man who had been leader for seven years of a party that was now the most widely popular party in the country was now, voluntarily, offering to let anyone have a go at him. The full Shakespearean tragedy of it all, disguised as comedy, was apparent. The nation, mesmerized, watched the cream pies being unpacked.

The Tories, because they have no nexus of responsibility, no knowledge of the rewards dangling just around the corner,

collapse into whimpering little bands of dissent when a leadership race develops — just *when* the attention of the country is riveted on them. At the one time when they should be
on their best behaviour, the bewildered voter sees them at
their worst — gleeful and grateful reporters, in print and on
TV, recording each pratfall. (The only people happier during
a Tory leadership fandango than media are the Liberals, who,
smiles as wide as their pork barrel, settle back to watch the
messy ruins, like a man sitting in his undershirt before the
TV set with a can of beer in his hand, fascinated by a demoli-
tion derby. The Grits actually despatch orders to their cabinet ministers to withhold any major announcements during
Tory internecine time, so that the front pages and the national news will be open and free for the follies that will inevi-
tably come.)

Liberals have been packing nomination meetings in Quebec for decades. It is why accidents never happen in their party;
the wrong candidate never gets the nomination, whereas the
approved choice, well greased and oiled for his future career
as a trained seal in the Grit backbench in Ottawa, has always
been properly raised in the party tradition — like mushrooms,
kept in the dark and fed plenty of horseshit.

The Tories simply don't know how to do the same things
with finesse. They are ham-handed, still apprentices after 116
years, not knowing how to conceal their tomfoolery. In the
run-up to the 1976 leadership convention, one Quebec riding
held its nomination meeting in a bar. The planned, quiet di-
vision of delegates between Clark and Mulroney forces was
suddenly reversed by a troop of motorcycle greasers supporting Claude Wagner.

One constituency chose its delegates at 11 AM in a senior
citizens' home. (After a protest, the voting was rescheduled
— for Christmas Day.) Another riding held its election at 2
PM on Grey Cup Day. And so it goes, the party with no visible
organization in Quebec, with only one of that province's
seventy-five MPs, sending from Quebec to each leadership
convention the second-highest number of delegates of any
province. There is something strange going on within

181

the cranium of the Conservative Party. Louis Riel must be giggling, wherever he is, in revenge.

The strain, the species, the bloodline, is growing weaker. The Tories are not even reproducing themselves in the IQ league. In 1967, when they replaced Dief, they had in the leadership race men of the calibre of Stanfield, Davie Fulton, Duff Roblin, Donald Fleming, Alvin Hamilton and Michael Starr — even leaving aside such as George Hees and Senator Wally McCutcheon.

In 1968, the Liberals had a substantial field of respected candidates challenging Pierre Trudeau for the leadership: Robert Winters, John Turner, Eric Kierans, Allan MacEachen, Paul Hellyer, Joe Greene — plus the too-old Paul Martin. In 1976, the Tories had what seemed like an even crop: Wagner, Mulroney, Flora MacDonald, Jack Horner, Clark, Sinc Stevens, Hellyer, plus the also-rans.

In 1983, after a sufficient period of seven years to develop worthy challengers to the tentative Clark, they entered the June convention with only three men who had any chance at all of winning — Crosbie, Clark and the man who wasn't even in the caucus, Mulroney. There was a fall of 543 votes on the first ballot from the *third* man, Crosbie, down to the inconsequential total of the fourth man, David Crombie. (The five bottom candidates *between* them got only 384 votes.) It doesn't say much for the regenerative powers of the party that had been muttering under its breath for seven years at the compromise choice of Joe.

Any national political party that can accommodate both Colin Kerr and Peter Pocklington as candidates for its highest office is worth writing a book about. Kerr, an ex-nightclub owner, the proprietor of a "magical" mynah bird named Rajah, declared early for the leadership, feeling his hour had come.

His platform was "quite simple. It's bee pollen. I plan to make a billion-dollar industry out of a bee pollen." How? By giving each of the 3,009 Tory convention delegates a bee-pollen pellet "for energy."

"The Dallas Cowboys take bee pollen. The president of the United States takes bee pollen" (one somehow does not doubt that). And Rajah takes bee pollen — as well as having fine political judgement.

"I was with Premier Davis on October 21, 1971," Kerr explained. "You can check the Hamilton *Spectator*. I bumped into Davis at a radio station and the bird just flew into his hand. Then he became premier." He also volunteers that Roy McMurtry "touched the bird" shortly before Davis named him Ontario attorney-general.

"Diefenbaker touched the bird. People tell me it was the first time he'd smiled since his wife Olive died. He told me: 'All I want to do is to touch Rajah, live one year and finish my memoirs.' And that's exactly what happened. These are factualities."

Rajah, by the way, had killed four of his last mynah bird mates. This would appear to make him a Tory too.

The facts are that Colin Kerr, along with mining promoter Terry Howes and retired contractor Alex Barker, who had lost his deposit in every election he had been in, did not make the cut, failing to ante up the five-thousand-dollar entrance fee and the required one hundred certified Tories to sign their nomination papers. Peter Pocklington, however, did.

Peter Puck was quite the most engaging and preposterous flake in recent years every to tarry in the upper reaches of a party that has included some first-class flakes. He is impossible to dislike, impossible to take seriously, a child-like faith in the verities of jungle warfare shining in his bright blue eyes. He is part Dale Carnegie, part positive thinking, part General Bullmoose.

Peter Puck grew up in London, Ontario, the dullest town in Canada since it is the headquarters of both the insurance industry and the Holiday Inn chain. It succeeds therefore in both the turgid and the tasteless. His father, naturally, was a prosperous insurance agent. Intent from childhood on being rich, young Peter used to sell his Christmas presents.

When he was five, he picked the chestnuts off a neighbour's lawn and sold them back to her. An entrepreneur at six, he filled his mother's fruit jars with cherries purloined from an orchard, added tap water and sold them door-to-door as "preserves." This, clearly, was the role model for Dennis the Menace. As a teenager, when his parents went on holiday, Pocklington knocked down the family barn and sold the lumber to Fidelity Trust—a company he would eventually own. He is a mystic and believes you can do "anything you want to do."

He is embarrassed by it now, and denies the story, but he once told reporter Linda Diebel that he is convinced he leaves his body on nocturnal flights to tour the Pyramids, to soar around the towers of the Kremlin or to swoop down the Nile. A candidate for leadership of the Progressive Conservative Party of all Canada is a married, rich Mackenzie King.

In person he is as soft as a cocker spaniel, with a gentle blond beard that makes him appear like a Hare Krishna beggar, all deep-dish sincerity and tail-wagging charm, on a street corner. He approached the goofy Tory race as he approaches all his business deals: "It's *all* just selling cars, only with more zeroes." He toys rather too much, in talk, with the strangely feminine gold bracelet that decorates his forearm.

The man who preached that what government needed was fiscal responsibility, in the middle of his leadership campaign lost $400,000, in jewellery and cash left on a bathroom counter, to thieves who jimmied the lock while Pocklington and his fashion-plate second wife Eva slumbered after watching his Edmonton Oilers in a Stanley Cup playoff game. Most of it was Mrs. Pocklington's diamond necklace and such like. The contribution of the putative future fiscally responsible prime minister was two thousand dollars in cash, mostly one-hundred-dollar bills.

In St. George, Ontario, during his campaign, Peter Puck told 160 party supporters that Indians should have been made "Canadian citizens" rather than allowed to establish reserves. "We can't protect people forever," he explained. "When the Romans took over an area, they immediately made the people citizens and taxed them 20 per cent. I'd do the same thing with Indians."

In one of the more bizarre events of a bizarre leadership race, Pocklington somehow persuaded Peter Regenstreif, a respected Canadian pollster who was a professor in New York State, to become a political adviser and thereby impair the credibility the professor might have as an objective political seer. He hired Skip Willis, a Toronto accountant who was son of a former Manitoba lieutenant-governor, and promised him a $43,000 Porsche 928-S (146 MPH) if he won the race.

Pocklington, along with John Gamble, debased the coinage of the whole Tory leadership struggle, since the media, obsessed with equal time, treated them as serious candidates and — in the column-inch ethic of fairness — gave them as much air time and space as if they were credible and serious contenders.

Gamble, in a prominent feature on the Op-Ed page of the Toronto *Star* ("If I Were PM") was asked, "Why do you think you can do a better job than Joe Clark?" and was allowed to reply: "Because I can do everything better than Joe Clark. Everything. *Everything.* I can do everything better than Joe Clark ever did. That's why I'm running. Anything and everything. I can inspire promises in the people and make promises that I could keep. I can show the kind of determination to do the job that the nation needs. There is nothing I can't do better than Joe Clark."

The question is whether John Gamble could *swim*.

Pocklington's main platform was a pledge to reform the tax system with a flat twenty-per-cent income tax across the board for everyone — then he revealed that he, as a millionaire, paid no income taxes at all, through the use of loopholes. He said, yes, a prime minister should be bilingual, while confessing he could not speak a word of French.

He started the Amway salesman scare, attending rallies of the super-patriot U.S.-based outfit in Edmonton, Moncton and Vancouver, urging the white-shoed salesmen to join the Tories. When they did commandeer one nominating meeting in Kamloops and capture two delegate spots, riding president Betty Thomas promptly fainted when she heard the voting results and then resigned along with her four senior executives.

There was Michael Wilson from Bay Street, tall, clean of

185

jaw, ponderous and so slow-moving that his wife revealed his mother was still arranging his dates when he was twenty-seven years of age. (Wilson and his mother denied it; his wife stuck by her story.)

One of the more bizarre moments of Canadian political history came during the candidates' debate a Toronto's Massey Hall when CTV's Pamela Wallin, the rising star in Canadian television, asked Wilson whether he was boring. Here was the poor man, live on television, actually attempting to explain that he is not boring while giving evidence of the fact at the same time.

Wilson arrived at a breakfast meeting in North Winnipeg to find only six Conservatives present. His bewildered campaign workers soon found that someone had phoned all the other guests to say the meeting had been cancelled.

It was hard to keep track of the zoo antics. In the middle of the campaign, the Quebec director of Joe Clark's campaign, Marcel Danis, was found to be in Tripoli as a guest of the government of Muammar Gadaffi, the sponsor of international terrorism. Before leaving, Danis told Canadian Press he was heading for Paris for a vacation after supervising the first forty-five Quebec delegate-selection meetings.

When the Mulroney forces were putting their troops in position, the question of Chateauguay riding came up. Robert Brunet, a lawyer with the Mulroney troupe, suggested as chief organizer a close friend and client, Dr. Denis Marsan, a dentist by profession, a town councillor in the town of Delson, member of the Optimist Club and generally accepted as a community leader.

The riding was controlled by René Delarue, a consulting engineer who by happenstance was finance director of Joe Clark's Quebec operation. The Clark people, as dirty in their operation — as they had to be — as the long-experienced Mulroney people, knew the vital factor was to call delegate meetings at the earliest possible date to prevent the Mulroney forces from getting organized.

In Chateauguay, the local riding association usually can count thirty members. By March 17, the cut-off date for signing new members, the ranks had swelled to six hundred, more than half of them teenagers. The innocent Marsan had never been involved in federal politics. But he did know his neighbourhood and set about door-knocking. On the Friday evening, his Mulroney supporters outnumbered the Clark people. Marsan's son Pierre recalled there was a lot of tension at the gathering, induced in part by two South Shore heavies who were muscling their way about, muttering threats.

The middle-class, middle-aged folk who entered the church basement meeting were given neat cards listing the pro-Clark delegates. But the packs of teenagers in the room overwhelmed them, and Denis Marsan snapped up all six delegates for his tiger.

After what they thought was a successful meeting, Dr. Marsan, his family and joyous organizers went off for the usual celebratory dinner. They returned, shortly after midnight, to their home in the small community near Candiac. When they opened the door, Mrs. Marsan went into hysterics.

Everything visible had been smashed. Water pipes had been cut. The kitchen was a mess, cupboards chopped up with an axe. Bedroom furniture was wrecked, clothes slashed with a knife. In the dental office, the x-ray machine had been smashed, records strewn about, the chair ripped — some $85,000 in damage overall.

"It's funny," recalled Richard Holden, a bon vivant lawyer friend of Mulroney's "that during the Cliche Royal Commission [the Quebec inquiry into construction violence, on which Mulroney was one of three commissioners] it turned out that most of the goons and thugs came from the South Shore. Do you suppose some of those people still hold a grudge against Brian?"

This is the way they play games in Quebec, where there are few Tories, but many Tory delegates to fight over. The Mulroney biters and slashers were generally from the old Tory guard — plus new and eager innocents like Dr. Marsan. The Clark troops, just as versed in a tire slash or misplaced ballot, were led by prominent faces from the old Union Nationale or from the Créditiste remnants.

Montreal's St. Jacques riding association met at the Ukrainian Hall on Centre Street in Point St. Charles, a notoriously down-at-the-gargle Montreal ward-heeler riding. The TV cameras just happened to be on hand to witness the arrival of twenty duly-accredited and weather-beaten residents of the Old Brewery Mission to vote for Mulroney, who took the slate by twenty-seven votes.

The celebrated Frank Hanley, a local political power, former member of the Quebec National Assembly and a city councillor, said, "They're conscientious electors. I hope there'll be some beer for them later." After the vote, cases of beer were carted in from the kitchen.

Rev. Bill McCarthy, director of the Old Brewery Mission, pointed out there were 194 people at the rally and only 212 bottles of beer were handed out — in fact there were even twenty-eight full bottles left over at the end of the gathering. (Mulroney's instant Tories were bused in by Uncle Harry's bus service. Clark's people used a Murray Hill bus to bring in thirty-two residents of an old folks' home, Residence Mont Carmel on Dorchester Boulevard. It was not determined if they were provided with free tea.)

The dashing Richard Holden, usually seen in the better Crescent Street bars, turned out to be legal adviser to the St. Jacques riding association for the meeting and accepted the men's credentials. At one point he *put* his hand gently on the arm of a masher who was wearing a Joe Clark sticker.

"Get your frigging hand *off* me," said the chap through his clenched teeth, "or I'll paste you through the door."

Holden, a man who delights, as all lawyers, in using the language once owned by Shakespeare, claims to have sweetly said, "Oh, yes, you're perfectly correct, sir. I shouldn't have done that. Now if we could discuss that matter . . . "

The watching nation loved the juicy spectacle. In St. Maurice riding, on the north shore of the St. Lawrence, halfway between Montreal and Quebec City, a meeting scheduled to begin at 8 PM Friday night didn't get underway until 2:30 AM Saturday morning because of procedural wrangling between Clark and Mulroney forces (in a province that elects just one Tory out of seventy-five seats).

In Champlain, a bus full of Mulroney supporters was stopped by toughs who threatened violence if the passengers

188

voted at the riding meeting. The Mulroney supporters never got off the bus. Clark backers swept all six delegate seats. In Toronto's York-Centre, Paul Harmes, age nine, his brothers Angelo, eleven, and Bill, thirteen, as card-carrying members of the Conservative Party helped elect two pro-Clark delegates. Their father is a senior delegate and Clark activist. (By this stage of the campaign, it was suggested the ideal delegate in Ottawa in June would be a ten-year-old wino.)

The birth of the "Ten-Minute Tories" was an outgrowth of Clark's efforts, since 1976, to attract younger people to an aging party. The party constitution was changed to allow Conservative campus clubs to send three delegates each to the leadership convention. With Clark and Mulroney manipulators leading the way, the number of clubs suddenly soared from 211 to 433. Party brass rejected almost half of them — including a club at a Newfoundland hairdressing school and one from an Alberta Mennonite Bible College. The names had been copied from an anti-abortion petition.

One of the campus clubs, formed March 11 at a Quebec City secretarial school, took just six minutes for its thirteen members to elect three Mulroney delegates. (Premier Richard Hatfield of New Brunswick says that, in truth, he was the original Tiny Tory, voting, at the age of nine, at the leadership convention that chose John Bracken in 1942.)

Such is the pull of eccentricity within the Tory psyche that even those not in the battle feel a need to make fools of themselves. As the real candidates recruited derelicts and bubblegummers in their struggle for a prime minister's chair, MP Allan Lawrence issued a strange press announcement from his office. It was to report that he decided *not* to run for the party leadership.

This was rather boggling (somewhat akin to Dr. Foth announcing he had decided not to run for secretary general of the United Nations), since there was no discernible brushfire sweeping the land in support of Mr. Lawrence's running for an office which he wouldn't have had a chance of winning. Politics is full of non-events, but this was a remarkable piece of non-news.

Pompous beyond recall, the announcement said he had

been weighing his chances since Clark resigned two months previous but cited western resentment against any Ontario candidate as the reason for his selfless decision to withdraw from a race he hadn't entered. Mr. Lawrence was unavailable for comment to reporters because, it turned out, he had left for Europe a week before his office sent out his pronouncement. It was the first case in history of a press release being issued by an answering service.

It was after midnight at Charlottetown airport and Joe Clark spied an employee in the hall. "Ah," says the candidate, "what's that you have in your hand?"

"It's a flashlight, sir."

"Ah, why are you carrying that?"

"Because it's dark outside."

Said Joe Clark, "Ah," — and he strode out purposely into the night.

Peter Puck, going nowhere rapidly, delighted the youngsters by showing up at the convention with his expensive chattel, Wayne Gretzky. Asked for his views, the wise young man, who looks so much like a blonde praying mantis when he skates, wisely said, "Since I am not familiar with the issues, it would be unwise for me to comment on them." The pity is that Peter Blaikie did not have the same initial introspection.

Blaikie, in a party of characters, is special. Tall, darkly handsome with suits that go out to here, a Rhodes Scholar, married to a statuesque psychiatrist, he would seem to have everything going for him. So intense that he constantly gives the impression of fighting off a swarm of bees even when at ease, he initiated a fight with the tender souls of the parliamentary press gallery within twenty minutes of being elected for a stormy term as president of the party.

He could invariably, in making a ten-minute speech in praise of Joe Clark, find some way to spend the first seven minutes talking about himself. Blaikie had lost twice in Lachine to Liberal Rod Blaker, a lawyer-turned-hotliner, himself well known — not just in the Commons as assistant deputy speaker — but also in the corridors on Parliament Hill, his ambition naked and scarcely concealed. (Not even a towel would encompass his ego.)

190

Blaikie, whose lust for Clark's job while he served him as president, was the more evident the more he denied it, put himself in the race and talked grandly about being the only real dark horse, a definite threat to be in third place after the first ballot.

The misplaced optimism seemed more than usually puzzling, since Clark and Mulroney, with their Tiny Tories and street-tough ploys, had carved up for themselves all of Quebec — Blaikie's only possible power base. No one could find any support for him across the country, where his frequent travels, when he was president, only served to export knowledge of his massive regard for his own abilities. Blaikie then provided more amusement for this trip along The Yellow Brick Road by suddenly announcing that he was withdrawing from the race because he realized he "wasn't familiar enough with the issues." The discovery that certain matters such as the Crow's Nest Pass freight rate mystery were beyond the ken of a Rhodes Scholar convinced him that he had best shuttle himself back to the sidelines.

How a past president of the party, who had travelled the land so assiduously, could not be familiar with the issues was a spectacle wondrous to behold. More jaundiced observers concluded that Blaikie, discovering to his mortification that he had no support, decided that piling up massive campaign debts wouldn't exactly be useful to his legal career. Mr. Blaikie, meet Mr. Gretzky.

And so it went, hearts and flowers abloom. Gamble, talking about the possibility that Clark might lose, said: "I hope it comes slowly. I hope it takes five ballots because I want to prolong Joe's agony. I want to chip away at him slowly. I want to hurt him just a little bit at a time." Delicious stuff! Harmony abounds. George Hees, who was prominent in the cabal that brought down Dief, danced a jig in Brian Mulroney's box when Clark lost on the fourth ballot, crying, "We've got him! We've got the S.O.B.!"

(Even the evangelists got swept up by the madness. Neal Fraser, the man who wanted to become leader because he feels the metric system is the most burning — and only — issue in the country, in his reference to abortion, in a speech to the national television audience, talked of "Solicitor Genital Robert Kaplan.")

The Tories shouldn't have been surprised at anything that happened to them on this site at Lansdowne Park, beside the Rideau Canal, the home of Ottawa's fairs, football, hockey and political immolations. Soon after the original Coliseum was built in 1903, its roof fell in from the weight of the snow. The next winter the roof collapsed again — for the same reason. In 1914, the boiler blew up, killing three men, twenty horses and six hundred head of poultry (it is not recorded how old the chickens were).

When Diefenbaker was crowned there in 1956, the Coliseum was still called the Cow Palace. The present Civic Centre, built as Ottawa's centennial project, includes the subterranean hockey rink whose roof is the grandstand for the football field. On the site in 1888, a Professor Williams ascended in a balloon, unfortunately dangling twenty-two year-old Tom Wensley at the end of a trailing rope. Just west of Bank Street the young man fell one thousand feet to his death.

In 1983, eager supporters of Joe Clark were discovered to have pasted pictures of their hero above the urinals in the men's washrooms. After the delegates had sweltered in the heat of June 11, with temperatures estimated at a hundred degrees on the convention floor, it turned out, embarrassed civic officials reported, that the enthusiastic campaign workers of the candidates, attempting to plaster the building with their signs, had covered the air-conditioning ducts with their propaganda.

14 The New Sheep

"There are worse things in the world than being a Scarecrow."

On the cement floor of the Ottawa Civic Centre, by late Saturday on June 11, 1983, there is an interesting mulch: squashed soft drink cans, masticated confetti, mangled posters, destroyed funny hats of destroyed (and funny) candidates, junk, paper, cardboard, mush, slop, goo. It is the detritus of democracy. Frank Lloyd Wright once said that if you imagined America as a table, and you tipped it up and all the debris fell to one side, that would be California. The floor of the Ottawa Civic Centre, supposedly the site of the anointing of the next Canadian prime minister, looked very much like what you would expect if you tipped over most of the waste baskets of a McDonald's Big-Mac parlour. The accredited inhabitants, manufacturers of the mulch, had just produced a made-to-order candidate.

Scuffing down in the debris, two remarkably resilient ladies danced the day and evening away. Kicking away the exhausted folding chairs, shuffling through the mangled remains of John Gamble's profile, they boogied — bodies in rhythm but minds elsewhere — to the frenetic beat of the house band, Ike Kelnick Express, and his electric organ (Ike's intention being musical, the ladies taking their own interpretation). They are, quite obviously, from Quebec, since the

Anglo-Saxon end of the country, being of the tight-assed heritage, somehow feels that two persons of the same sex dancing together signifies something squirrely.

The ladies, both being of what is called an uncertain age — one in bright red, the other in the spaghetti straps that an observer thought had disappeared after his high school prom — in fact epitomize this coronation. Ignored, blissful in their isolation down in one corner of the arena they represent the element that controlled this convention: the province with the most powerful purchasable votes that has the least possible influence on the Conservative Party of Canada.

It is as if the Natural Governing Party, in full command of its faculties, had decided to pluck a champion from the Northwest Territories. Or, perhaps even more incongruous, from the sheikdom of Fortress Alberta, where seldom has been heard an encouraging word about a Grit since Jean Chrétien — who with his pea-soup accent confirms in the Rugged West mind what Johnny Baptiste is all about.

(The only thing that keeps this country — the second-largest land mass of ignorance on earth — together is its blissful lack of knowledge of its disparate parts. Does the USSR's Georgia know about Siberia? Does the Ukraine know anything about the treasures of French art hidden in the Hermitage in Leningrad? Of course not. Canada should relax and enjoy the luxury of geographical dissimilitude. I digress.)

Is politics in Quebec of a different breed? On the Friday night before the vote, a heavy operative from Montreal who has some knowledge of money received a phone call after midnight in his Chateau Laurier room. The caller, since they did not have to be introduced, said he needed by morning two thousand dollars in small bills — small bills being twenties, small bills not being able to be traced. The recipient smiled and politely hung up. He could not acquire, after midnight, two thousand dollars in small bills. But he knew others who could. Politics is managed differently on the other side of the Ottawa River, and the Tories, finally in 1983, were learning the ropes. Sir John A. would have understood.

Brian Mulroney knew he had won the Conservative leadership the moment he walked into the Ottawa Civic Centre

194

on Saturday, June 11, and spotted the Harder family and their friends. He knew because they had driven all the way in a camper truck from Williams Lake, high in the Cariboo cattle country of the interior of British Columbia to vote for him and attempt to bring down the man they called The Wimp. They parked the camper in the parking lot of the Civic Centre and drank rye and ginger between votes and watched the proceedings on a portable Panasonic.

Ron Harder serves as Cariboo-Chilcotin riding president for both the federal Tories and the provincial Social Credit. He liked Mike Wilson first and John Crosbie a bit. But Wilson, when he came through Williams Lake, seemed a bit too much Bay Street.

Then came Mulroney and wife Mila, doing their subterranean campaign strategy of capturing the "boonies." Harder remembers: "It was just so low key. Just the two of them and they stayed overnight. We just sat around the kitchen talking — you know what I mean?" Harder and wife Muriel and youth delegate Camilla Belsher voted for Mulroney and drank rye with their friends Don and Marnie Adamski while their kids played on the asphalt. Mulroney won it with bits of loyalty brought in a camper truck all the way from Williams Lake, B.C.

He won because he had the money to do the polling that told him, consistently, that his real threat, Crosbie, could get more than 600 to 650 votes on the first ballot — meaning he wouldn't have enough ballots to make up the difference from a base that low. (Crosbie got 639.) The Mulroneyites for weeks tried to tell that to any reporter who didn't want to listen. When their lack of interest became dangerous, the Mulroney camp leaked a poll showing those projections to the *Globe and Mail*.

(As part of Dr. Foth's vain attempts to save the nation from itself, in the three hours that it took the slow-footed Tories to count the first ballot, I ran a pool — at two dollars a pop — as to the eventual winner and his winning vote. There were 108 entries, practically every recognizable national journalist in the country — newspaper, magazine, TV, radio — plus back-room boys and prominent fringe players.

195

(It indicated an interesting tone. Mulroney is not generally liked by the press, regarded as too slick and too sensitive to criticism. The droll Crosbie is extremely hard to dislike, dispensing quotable quotes like sheep droppings. Only forty-one of the nation's experts picked Mulroney; sixty-seven of them picked either Crosbie or Clark, Crosbie getting the majority of those votes. When it gets right down to the wire, the hardened, cynical press votes not with its head but its heart. The winner? With Mulroney's exact final count of 1,585 votes? Southam News' Aileen McCabe, who covered Mulroney as her campaign beat, saw his sly strategy at first-hand and had been privately touting him all the way in office bets.)

Mulroney himself confessed later that he probably couldn't have won a last-ballot showdown with Crosbie — the man who impaled himself on his tongue in the final weeks of the campaign. John Crosbie is possibly the most interesting man to enter federal politics since Pierre Trudeau, a man whose agile tongue flaps like a seal flipper, gives the appearance of an out-of-work butcher but is as arrogant as they come. "John Crosbie," said his enemy Joey Smallwood, "isn't a Liberal. He isn't a Tory. He's simply a Crosbie and that's what he'll always be."

For all his casual air, Crosbie has tried to run everything he has been connected with. He tried to overthrow Smallwood as head of the Newfoundland Liberals. Fought off, he formed his own reform party, which didn't work. He switched to the Tories and was the real brains and workhorse behind the raffish charmer, Frank Moores, who wanted to keep the premier's post for himself.

Foiled again, Crosbie moved on to Ottawa, to "bood-get" fame and wary nervousness from Clark, who shunted him into the dead-end External Affairs shadow-cabinet post once Crosbie told him, quite honestly, that he would be going for the leadership if and when it ever came open.

Born to wealth and a fine mind, Crosbie moves through life with the usual assurance that comes from both. (Wife Jane is the wittiest wife on Parliament Hill. When the Clark government foundered on her husband's budget, she cracked,

"The operation was a success, but the doctor died."] Crosbie's problem is that he is quite aware he has the finest mind in the Tory caucus, where he has few friends and had a surprisingly thin backing in the leadership contest. An inherently shy man, he has a disconcerting habit, when talking to you, of rolling his eyes upward and avoiding contact, as if, observed one reporter, "he was studying the insides of his eyelids." There is the suspicion among some that he is in fact as cold and aloof in his real persona as Pierre Trudeau.

Crosbie, of course, killed himself (if there was any doubt he was a Tory, he removed it here) by his casual slur in Quebec. He had been making rather good progress with the point that he "like 22 million other Canadians" was unilingual. No one else had ever had the guts to say that in public before: that nowhere near the five million people in Quebec were bilingual and he shouldn't be regarded as "a criminal" because he wasn't.

It was fair comment, gaining him a lot of points from sensible people who had never quite had the courage to say that themselves. We can't leave the running of the country completely to a "bilingual élite," he said, pushing his advantage just a trifle bit further, an interesting concept that had been bothering a number of Canadians for years.

That was the casual, sensible, honest Crosbie at his best. Pushed even further, nagged by basically anglophone reporters who sniffed a little blood, the unfortunate aspect of the Brahmin Crosbie burst forth, testily. Out came the fatal riposte that he couldn't speak "Chinese or German either," but that didn't prevent him or other Canadians from communicating with those nations.

It was a remark, under examination, so insensitive as to reveal a man who had never really thought seriously about Quebec or its yeasty role in this dull country. There is this analogy, you see, between Ludwig van Beethoven and John Crosbie. Imagine Beethoven applying for a job as a music critic. He could cite his great success as a composer and an expert on music. He would have only one handicap as critic: he was deaf.

Crosbie, while becoming a gold medallist at Queen's and Dalhousie and acquiring experience in senior positions at the municipal, provincial and federal levels that dwarfed his rivals, in his easy arrogance on the way to the top never bothered to consider Lester Pearson's warning that he would be Canada's last unilingual prime minister. From that point on, the big Newf didn't have a chance.

In fact, he had one left. It was Joe Clark, the man who had tried too much too soon — seduced by the obviously flawed competition that presented itself in 1976. There were those of us fascinated by trying to insert ourselves into the Clark headbone (and that of Maureen) after the third ballot in that steamy cauldron of the Ottawa rink in June.

Clark was obviously going nowhere after the first ballot, dropping a telling six votes from 1,091 to 1,085 on the second round, down further to 1,058 on the third ballot as Mulroney rushed ever higher. As columnist Charles Lynch had told a university paper before the convention: "Joe has a basic weakness that doesn't show up in the polls. People may go up and say, 'Oh shit, not again.' "

Clark had a choice. He could have gone to Crosbie before the final ballot in an attempt to block Mulroney, a man he had known since he was seventeen and for whom he had no respect. Just as Mulroney privately views Clark as a man with no street smarts and no accomplishments in real life, Clark regards Mulroney as an opportunist, a man with style and no substance.

If Clark had gone to Crosbie, a supremely confident man of superior intellect who has a gritty, Churchillian nub to him, he might have anointed a man who could be prime minister for decades.

If Clark stayed still, thus killing any Crosbie chance, he knew the new leader — and supposedly prime minister — would be Mulroney, a man he suspected would be caught out on his shallowness by the Liberals and the electorate, leaving Joe Clark the eventuality, in the British tradition, of a second (third?) chance down the pike. Clark, as a man who loves the Commons and knows no other trade, might be content to wait out his time there and observe, quietly, the fate of the charming Irish neophyte who knew none of the arcane House rules Clark had memorized backwards.

Nancy Jamieson, the shrewd Clark aide who moved on to the office of Bill Davis, thinks otherwise. Though a loyal Clark operative through the convention, she knew it was over after the first telling ballot. (Her job was to fib to Clark's mother that everything was okay.) She says, ruefully, "There'll be no second chance for Joe. The public has made up its mind. It's sort of like running into a bad lay on the street, the day after. You just don't know what to say. It's embarrassing."

Senator Lowell Murray, the guru who has led Clark into so many of his bad decisions, agrees. "He's finished as an active politician. He has to find something else."

As the drained delegates waited in the fetid air for the fated total fourth ballot count, the result inevitable, the amazed Mulroney forces suddenly saw Clark and his entourage moving through the melée towards their box at the opposite end of the arena. Stunned, they checked their communications. No, Clark had not phoned on the telephone connection between the two boxes, had not sent a runner with any message. As it turned out, Clark—with some class—merely wanted to shake Mulroney's hand as a gesture of solidarity before the final result. But Mulroney at that moment was sitting naked in hockey dressing room 60 down below, having showered, and was preparing his acceptance speech. Mila Mulroney was half-dressed. Joe Clark, awkward to the end, arrived at Mulroney's box, the nation's television sets watching in wonder, to find no one there. Said a Mulroney aide, disgusted at the Clarkian foul-up, "Typical."

There was a final moment of concern for Mulroney's Quebec men when they detected some movement among Clark's Quebec delegates. Sensing defeat, some Clark supporters seemed likely to move to Mulroney on the third ballot so as to be on the winning team. It could have dropped Clark to third and forced a Mulroney-Crosbie showdown on the final ballot. "That's the last thing we wanted," explained a Mulroney strategist. Senator Guy Charbonneau and Michel

Cogger, Mulroney's key people, moved quickly to keep Clark's support steady. Instructed Cogger to his Quebec contacts in the Clark camp: "You stick with your chicken until he's fried."

At the final count — Clark 1,325, Mulroney 1,585 — Mila Mulroney from Yugoslavia threw herself on the neck of her husband who still gives the appearance of just being off the boat from Ireland. By now in their box were the Newfoundland forces, including Crosbie's bright assistant Ross Reid, who lost seventy pounds *before* the campaign in the knowledge he had better look svelte and businesslike before the nation's cameras, and who emerged a very good-looking young man. "I," he announced, half in exhaustion and half in exultation at his new body, "am now going to screw my way across Europe."

The next evening Joe and Maureen sat in their living room at Stornoway, numb with the hurt. The phone rang and Maureen went to answer. She came back to announce, "The Joe Clark headquarters is burning down." They sat silent, looking at the wall, for fifteen minutes. The end really had come.

15 The Life of Brian

"I found myself in the midst of a strange people,
who, seeing me come from the clouds, thought I was
a great Wizard. Of course I let them think so,
because they were afraid of me, and promised to do
anything I wished them to."

On July 10, 1975, after Robert Stanfield had signalled his decision to step down, I wrote a newspaper column running over the possible successors. It didn't look impressive: Lougheed reluctant, Wagner too flawed, Horner too rough, Pat Nowlan too noisy, Joe Clark "too young." Instead, I suggested, the stumbling Tories should select someone I had never met, a chap named Brian Mulroney out of Montreal.

Some weeks later, I received a phone call in Vancouver from Montreal. It was Mulroney. "When did you decide to run?" I asked.

"The second time I read it in your column," he said. He was indeed the Candidate from Whimsy.

It took the Tories seven years to accept Dr. Foth's counsel, but at least they took it — which is more than one can say about the ungrateful Grits, who churlishly ignored my free advice. It is not clear why Dr. Foth has to save the Conservatives from themselves but, God knows, somebody has to.

Martin Brian Mulroney wafts charm like after-shave lotion. His voice comes out of the bottom of a rain barrel. The jaw is from Gibraltar. It is typical of the Tories, after complaining for seven years that they had a leader with no chin, they chose a man who has enough for two. When they make the movie of Robert Redford's life, Mulroney is going to play Redford.

The only thing longer than his jaw is his ambition. Conrad Black, who has known him for years, says the thing that sets Mulroney apart is that "he's like a Liberal. He's devious and scheming. He's been planning this for twenty years." Too much ambition in the Tory party, as we know, is regarded as something not quite cricket, just as the British, preferring amiable amateurs, look with dark suspicion on professionals in any field.

The boy from Baie Comeau, once past the charm, can be a rough customer. Several years ago, when asked how he would handle the political challenge of Pierre Trudeau or René Lévesque, he responded immediately: "You see that hallway down there? He's down at that end, I'm up at this end. I'll meet him halfway. And if that's not good enough, I'll kick him in the nuts."

He's a sentimental glutton for work, his Irishness sticking to him like smoke in a peat bog. When Colonel Robert McCormick, owner of the Chicago *Tribune*, who established Baie Comeau as a newsprint supply, came to town, nine-year-old Brian would stand on the piano and sing "Dearie" in his boy soprano. He was rewarded with fifty dollars in crisp bills, which he would promptly turn over to his mother. Today Mulroney can sing, at a party, every one of the songs made famous by Vera (Sweetheart of the Forces) Lynn in her weepy *Hits of the Blitz* album.

His balance wheel is wife Mila, a vivacious five-foot ten-inch lady who at thirty is fourteen years his junior (the same age difference that separates Joe Clark and Maureen McTeer). She is as basic as the Yugoslavia of her origin. Her father, Dr. Dmitri Pivnicki, came to Canada twenty-four years ago as an intern. He is now head of psychiatry of Montreal's Royal Victoria Hospital and treated Margaret Trudeau when she checked herself into that hospital. Mila was just three courses short of her engineering degree when the persuasive Mulroney, who discovered her in a bikini at age eighteen beside the pool at the Mount Royal Tennis Club, took her to the altar instead.

202

(During the leadership campaign, advisers told her to junk most of her rings when she visited small towns — but put on diamonds when she hit Alberta.)

There's a dark side to that Irish soul. He is a curious mixture of sweet talk and harsh talk. David Humpreys, Clark's close friend, says, "Mulroney the inveterate and almost irresistible charmer becomes sour and suspicious when that charm is resisted or rejected."

He was bitter beyond belief when his audacious try for the leadership in 1976 was rejected — he only thirty-seven with no Commons seat, trying a *coup d'état* from the outside. Known as the Bionic Man by the press, he destroyed himself with a wooden, overwritten speech that was crafted in pre-convention days by a brains trust hidden away in Magog in Quebec's Eastern Townships. The rumour around the cottages of Magog was that the chap's head was unzipped after breakfast, the bionic brain was shipped across to the brain trust's cottage and stuck with principles. It was sent back for lunch, retrieved in the afternoon and returned safely for cocktails.

Insiders suspect Mulroney never disclosed his 1976 campaign expenses because he was bankrolled by corporate giants Paul Desmarais and Charles Bronfman — both Liberals and friends of Trudeau. He had guaranteed their anonymity. It would not have looked good if two Trudeau supporters and money men had been listed as his major donors.

Mulroney, going down behind Wagner and Clark in 1976, complained to reporters he had been the victim of a gang-up (or, as Charlotte Gobeil told her TV listeners, "a gangbang.") His bitterness centred on the fact that he was painted as a slick outsider, with no party loyalties, when in fact he had been working the party ropes in Quebec since the age of seventeen.

The Jaw That Walks Like a Man began to drink too much, worrying his friends with the time spent in the Maritime Bar in the basement of the Ritz-Carlton Hotel, which is right across fashionable Sherbrooke Street from the offices of the Iron Ore Company of Canada, where he had assumed the presidency from William Bennett, one of whose daughters he used to take out.

Mulroney and Clark, for all their mutual displays of admiration, loathe each other. In private, Mulroney was scalding and scathing in his opinion of his new leader, meanwhile professing loyalty in public. He slipped just once, when he relaxed in his Westmount home with a free-lance writer, Stephen Kimber, apparently assuming his remarks were off the record.

The damaging article, in the June 1978 issue of *Financial Post* magazine, had Mulroney saying, "I didn't run for the leadership because I needed a house," an obvious reference to Clark's move from an Ottawa apartment to Stornoway, the official residence of Opposition leaders. "I already had a house. And I didn't run because I needed a job. I had a good job. I ran because the Conservative party needed a winner."

Early in 1981, his bitterness finally dissipating, Mulroney obviously took a look at his lifestyle and his desires to have another go at Mr. Clark's shaky crown. He hasn't had a drink for more than two years. It's soda water over ice every time. One Montreal observer (not a total fan), says, "It shows the determination and strength in the man to give it up, zap, like that. I've never met a man who has singularly wanted something so badly as Brian wanted to beat Joe."

He mainlines on two packs of du Maurier and twenty cups of coffee every day. Will he survive Question Period without a cigarette break?

Mulroney's relentless ambition does have a *Liberal* ring to it. If he had stayed in Quebec he undoubtedly would have become a Liberal — the route to the top in that province — like his electrician father. But by going away to university at St. Francis Xavier in Antigonish, Nova Scotia, he came under the ambit of the Stanfield influence and became a Tory instead. He certainly was no one-dimensional man, his potential shown in this description in the university yearbook: "Silver-tongued orator . . . undefeated in three intercollegiate debates . . . President of Maritime Progressive Conservative Student Federation . . . Prime Minister of Maritime University Students' Parliament . . . chaired Hungarian Relief Committee . . . winner of three campus oratorical contests . . . dramatic talents shown in *Caine Mutiny* and *Everyman* . . . member of Honour Committee . . . athletic abilities displayed in interclass hockey and football . . . "

He has been treated somewhat unfairly about his reluctance to run. The Irish Sammy Glick from Baie Comeau always wanted financial stability first. He had just been admitted to the Bar when his father died in 1965. The young lawyer moved his mother, sixteen-year-old brother and twelve-year-old sister into a Montreal apartment and supported them. He did not get married until he was thirty-four. Finding a seat for a Tory in Quebec, for an anglophone even though bilingual, is something akin to a Liberal seeking an opening in Alberta. He has bided his time and — because of the weakness of his opponents — pulled it off.

The tweedy Tories, the party of supposed unsophistication, in fact did a most remarkable thing. The party that is at its lowest ebb in electoral strength in Quebec has chosen its first leader in ninety-two years from that strange, forbidding province.

The Tories may just have signalled something to the nation with their choice of Jaws II. They had before them the formidable figure of John Crosbie, a man who probably could have made an admirable prime minister, a man with a fine mind and a wit as homey and comfortable as a gumboot.

The brave and adventuresome decision of the Tory party (of supposed Bay Street, or supposed Prairie red-neckism) is going to have a considerable effect on the country. The party has bitten the bullet — thanks in part to Joe Clark — and has said that it will not abide any longer a leader who has not taken the trouble to make himself bilingual.

It has, in truth, advertised that however bright its leading figures, however qualified, those aspirants had better make sure in the future they have taken the trouble to equip themselves to speak to the one-quarter of Canada that is francophone (especially when there is a government in that province that wants to separate). That is courageous, when you think about it; telling a highly-qualified Crosbie that it would like him, really — if only he had taken the trouble to understand this country a little better.

There's going to be a trickle-down from the Tory decision to go with the Candidate from Whimsy. It fulfills Pearson's warning. It signals to all the aspiring and bright young people around the country that French indeed is important, when even the neanderthal Tories make a conscious decision to pick an unelected bilingual leader over a vastly more experienced, unilingual candidate. It will show in the enrolment in the bilingual programs in the anglophone areas of the country, and was probably the most telling experience in the country since passage of the Official Languages Act.

That legislation was a diktat from Trudeau. Choosing Mulroney was a conscious, open decision by 3,006 Tory delegates, most of whom can't speak a word of French. They showed tolerance and they showed shrewdness. John Crosbie will wait his turn. Martin Brian Mulroney will set an example.